Football Brands

Football Brands

Sue Bridgewater

Warwick Business School,
University of Warwick, UK

palgrave
macmillan

First published 2010 by
PALGRAVE MACMILLAN

Palgrave Macmillan in the UK is an imprint of Macmillan Publishers Limited, registered in England, company number 785998, of Houndmills, Basingstoke, Hampshire RG21 6XS.

Palgrave Macmillan in the US is a division of St Martin's Press LLC, 175 Fifth Avenue, New York, NY 10010.

Palgrave Macmillan is the global academic imprint of the above companies and has companies and representatives throughout the world.

Palgrave® and Macmillan® are registered trademarks in the United States, the United Kingdom, Europe and other countries

ISBN 978-0-230-23253-2

This book is printed on paper suitable for recycling and made from fully managed and sustained forest sources. Logging, pulping and manufacturing processes are expected to conform to the environmental regulations of the country of origin.

A catalogue record for this book is available from the British Library.

A catalog record for this book is available from the Library of Congress.

10 9 8 7 6 5 4 3 2 1
19 18 17 16 15 14 13 12 11 10

Printed and bound in Great Britain by
CPI Antony Rowe, Chippenham and Eastbourne

In memory of my parents, June and Gordon Hallard

CONTENTS

FIGURES AND TABLES

Figures

Tables

ACKNOWLEDGMENTS

The writing of this book on football brands would not have been possible without the kind help and access that has been provided by a number of football clubs, football bodies, and other knowledgeable individuals within the football field.

I am extremely grateful for the assistance and cooperation of Manchester United Football Club. Specifically David Gill and Philip Townsend gave generously of their time and guidance in the writing of the case study about their club and provided me with valuable insights. Without them the case study would not have been completed. At the League Managers Association, Richard Bevan, Jim Souter, and Graham Mackrell were helpful as ever, and gave insights into the brand challenges for football brands. Thanks to Verity Dodd, Pauline Healer and all involved in Sunderland's (successful!) World Cup Bid 2018 and 2022 at Sunderland AFC and Sunderland City Council for allowing me to include a case about a club and city which will always be close to my heart. Might I also thank everyone at the Football Association for involving me in research projects over the years which have helped me to explore the national and international dimension of the England football brand.

Many others helped with information, by providing useful articles and copies of their work. I am grateful to them all for their time and cooperation. Any errors or omissions are the responsibility of the author.

Sue Bridgewater

Why view football clubs and organizations as brands?

The purpose of this book is to help readers to understand why brands are important, why football clubs, football bodies, players, and tournaments are increasingly talked about in terms of brands, and the ways in which they differ and must be managed differently from other types of brands. The book combines real case histories of football brands and the challenges which they face with a reflection on what we can learn from theory in the areas of both branding and sports marketing.

The book begins with a discussion of the reasons for considering football clubs, football bodies, players, and tournaments as brands, and what insights can be gained from viewing all of these as football brands.

Why are brands important?

Marketers argue that brands are important on a number of levels. First, brands make a financial contribution to firms. Up to 70 percent of a firm's earnings can be attributed to brands (Perrier 1997). Brands did not use to be mentioned in financial statements, but increasingly their value is recognized among the "intangible assets" of firms. Moreover, whilst the average British and American company is valued by the stock market at twice net balance sheet assets, companies with strong brands are valued at four times net assets (*Financial Times* 1991). Nestlé paid £2.5 billion to acquire Rowntree (with its portfolio of brands such as KitKat, Smarties, and Polo mints), six times the value of the net assets of Rowntree (Doyle 2002). Second, customers build loyalty to strong brands. The decision to buy a Mercedes or a Ferrari confers much more than the ability to travel between places: the customer is buying a set of attributes, such as reliability or speed, and associations, such as prestige and status, which they – and others whose opinion they value – perceive in the brand.

Finally, brands now provide the guiding principles for market-oriented organizations. Over time, research attention has shifted from a focus on brand image (Boulding 1956) to the creation of brand identity (Kapferer 1997; Harris and de Chernatonay 2001). Brand image is concerned with understanding what customers value in a brand, whilst brand identity also encompasses the process of ensuring that employees' values and behavior toward customers and other stakeholders are consistent with these aspects.

Why football brands?

Given the importance of brands to marketers and in business, it is perhaps not surprising that recent decades have seen the study of brands in a broader range of organization types or sectors. Charities, the public sector, and e-marketers all seek to build brands with which customers and potential customers can identify.

The sporting world has long recognized the fervent loyalty of fans to particular sporting stars and teams. The media abounds with images of crowds turning out to greet David Beckham and his England teammates in Japan during the 2002 World Cup, the passion of Liverpool FC's Kop singing "You'll never walk alone," or the amazing 40,000 fans whom, despite a difficult season for all concerned with the club, Luton Town FC recently took with them to the Johnstone's Paint Trophy Final at Wembley stadium.

At the same time, the commercial significance of sport as a sector, and football in particular, has continued to grow apace in the last decade.

Sport is a significant sector in economic, social, and management terms. Globally, the market alone is estimated to be worth around $12 billion per annum (Ozanian 2005).

Within the United Kingdom, Sport England estimated the sport market at around £21.2 billion in 2008 and growing, even in a time of recession. Football (known as soccer in the United States) is one of the most globally significant sports. While many sports have appeal and commercial success within particular regions, such as baseball and ice hockey in North America, few appeal to fans in all regions of the world. Some commentators point to the different profile of football in the United States – it is a participation sport and is popular with women players, while the men's game predominates in other regions. Commercially, however, Major League Soccer in the United States attracts more fans (more revenue) than does the National Hockey League (NHL), and so the sport must be viewed as globally attractive. Certainly, Manchester United, Chelsea, Real Madrid, and other big football clubs attract the loyal support of fans on a global scale.

To what extent, though, should global sports clubs be viewed as brands and even global brands?

Even the mention of brand in conjunction with football is likely to raise the hackles of many football fans. Brand does not, however, necessarily mean commercial. Charities, public institutions, cities, and countries may consider themselves as brands. From a marketing perspective, branding is as much about evaluating what is important to the people with whom the brand engages, and making sure that the organizations' values are aligned, than it is about commercial development. To consider football clubs, football bodies, football competitions, and initiatives as brands, is at least to engage in a discussion about what they stand for, what is integral to these brands, and how best they should behave and communicate to be clear, consistent, and in service of their "customers."

For these reasons, considering football clubs and other football organizations as brands – and seeing what insights can be gained from doing so – may be a useful exercise even for those who deplore the commercialization of football.

Sports marketing theory argues strongly that football and other sports clubs should be considered as brands. These arguments focus on a number of attributes of sports clubs that make this appropriate. First, the media interest in sports clubs means that they have an increasing awareness of image.

Certainly, sports attract loyal, even fanatical, support. Within sports marketing literature there is a growing volume of work in the areas of "fan identification," or the relationships that fans have with clubs (Lascu et al. 1995; Wann 1995; Sutton et al. 1997) and with loyalty to particular teams or sports personalities (Fullerton 1995; Wakefield and Sloan 1995).

The growing commercial importance of sport means that

clubs are increasingly concerned with raising revenue in order to successfully meet their sporting aims. For a football club this may be how it might attract greater numbers of fans in attendance at matches or events. For a football body (see the LMA case study, page 50) this might be to provide a better service to members of the association, or otherwise help the football body to meet the needs of its members.

Sports theory also explores why fans support a specific club or sports star, what influences the choices they make, and what would prompt them to spectate or participate more in particular sports. Hence sports clubs are increasingly engaging in research and activities that marketers would recognize as market research and market analysis.

The issues that clubs are addressing include decisions on location – commercialization of sports recognizes the importance of stadia in revenue generation, and so football clubs are tending to build bigger and better stadia to capitalize on the possibilities. Clubs are also looking at the demographic profile of fans, and making pricing decisions that may encourage the involvement of future fans. Clubs may differentiate the offer of tickets and other hospitality at matches between fans with different profiles. In other words, clubs are splitting into groups or segmenting their fan base, and designing marketing strategies and altering the marketing mix (price, place, promotion, service) offered to different types of fans.

In all of these senses, it would appear that football as a business views clubs and individuals as brands around which marketing strategies and marketing mix activities occur.

This book focuses on the view that football clubs, football bodies, football competitions, and football players are in effect football brands, and that this merits further discussion to see what useful insights can be gained into how they work, how they can be marketed effectively, and how they differ from other types of brands.

Today's key branding challenges

In any sector, success begins with an understanding of markets and environment. What are the emerging needs of customers, and what are the possibilities for developing effective solutions to these needs? The current market environment can be described as one in which the following apply.

- **Rising customer expectations:** Increasing competition and global over-supply in many sectors has resulted in consumers expecting more. Customers expect greater value from their suppliers in terms of lower prices and higher quality, and often solutions that are tailored to their individual needs.
- **Speed of change:** More and more markets are becoming like the fashion industry, with customers expecting a continual series of new models. Change affects not only the products and services but also the channels through which these are delivered to market. IT and electronic marketing are creating opportunities for new entrants to find new, cheaper, and more effective means of delivering value to customers.
- **Blurred boundaries:** Boundaries that used to create barriers to new entrants and limit competition in particular markets are eroding. First, globalization means that buyers and competitors no longer recognize geographic limits, but search for the best around the globe. Advances in technology make it easier to offer access to products and services worldwide. Second, the boundaries between industries are disappearing. Retail banking services might be offered by banks and financial service institutions but also by supermarkets and players from quite different sectors. Both the food industry and pharmaceuticals are producing "healthy eating" products, and new categories such as "nutriceuticals" are emerging.

The importance of brands

In this rapidly changing world, continued success depends on developing new products and services, new channels, and new markets. While leaders and organizations have vision that may enable them to determine their strategic direction, the organization needs to align to deliver on its value propositions. This alignment can be achieved in uniting behind brand personalities and promises. Brands have personalities, and represent the "identity" behind which organizations align to deliver on their brand promises and create powerful assets.

What does this mean for football?

Fans as customers

The identification of fans with their cherished club is more emotional than rational. For many brands, customers may be attracted by a mix of rational and emotional criteria. In most instances, the emotional ties, which could be father or mother–child, regional affiliation, or support of a star player, are in large measure emotional rather than rational.

As in any other sector, the customers of football brands exist in a world in which the following apply.

Rising expectations

Fans are the mainstay of football. Without fans, local or in some cases global, there would be no revenue from match attendance, merchandise sales, broadcast revenue, or value for corporate organizations that sponsor teams. Football fans are, however, a unique and particularly demanding set of "customers."

Not only do fans expect value, their expectations may be un-realistic. Exceed expectations and remain in the Premier League one year, and the club's fans will be envisaging European qualification in the following season. This expectation can place pressure on clubs, football managers, and players, which may be counterproductive.

Perhaps more than any other sector, football fans have opti-mistic, perhaps unreasonable, expectations of the level their chosen team can achieve. They may respond to an excellent performance by contacting radio phone-ins and web forums demanding that the club "push on" and buy better players to sustain and improve this performance, regardless of whether this is realistic given the financial resources of the club.

Speed of change

Increased mobility of football players, as a result of increased player power, the role of agents, and the Bosman ruling, mean that more and more players play for clubs briefly before moving on. In addition, the tenure of football managers is declining, as pressure to deliver against fan expectations mounts. Football has always been a game in which one season's heroes may be next season's "zeroes." If anything the speed of change in football is accelerating.

Blurred boundaries

Football is an increasingly global game. Its interconnection with other national football associations, involvement in international competitions, and regulation by regional and global football authorities, mean that a football league or association does not operate in isolation. Football is now a business, as well as a "beautiful game," such that its clubs, bodies, and players are stakeholders in a bigger network, which expands well beyond the confines of the game itself. Indeed, the more the game develops commercially, the more an understanding of other businesses, which are linked to football through sponsorship, corporate hospitality, or in response to the increased celebrity of football players and managers, becomes essential to understanding the bigger picture surrounding football.

Importance of brands

Football clubs attract global levels of support. Football clubs such as Manchester United, Real Madrid, and AC Milan, at a league level the English Premier League and the Spanish La Liga, and at an individual level players such as Kaká, Ronaldo, and Ji-Sung Park, all have significant numbers of fans in all parts of the world. While the game is governed by many of the same rules as 50 years ago, in other respects it is unrecognizable. It now involves multi-million-pound takeovers, global owners, major brands drawing from a global pool of talent, and access to match coverage and club information via satellite television, the Internet, and even in prospect, the concept of playing competitive matches in international markets. Although some deplore the impact of business on football, football continues its "outstanding commercial and financial growth" (Deloitte and Touche 2009), and the unprecedented and relentless pace of change in the football business continues.

Global or local?

As big clubs get richer and more global, those with lesser resources struggle to compete and sometimes even to survive. While fans press clubs to move on, gain promotion, buy better players, a marketing perspective has enabled some clubs to appreciate that their priority should be to develop as local brands. For these brands, the greatest appeal, the best relationships, and in turn the greatest potential revenue sources, lie in their local communities. While broader appeal may be gained via digital media, these relationships should not be neglected in pursuit of success.

Highly involved stakeholders

Many fans eat, breathe, and sleep their clubs. Their interest and the emotional bond that they have with a club, its players, manager, and all that surrounds the club, transcends the level of involvement that most customers have even in their favorite products or services. Even the most loyal fan of a particular beer, chocolate bar, or cup of coffee might experiment with a different brand to try something new, or if the previous brand disappoints over a period of time. But would a fan change allegiance to a rival team? Not even if the club underperforms over a period of years or suffers successive relegations. Fans do sometimes distance themselves from football brands if they underperform (see Chapter 2, page 67, and Chapter 6, page 169), but they do not switch allegiance to other brands.

Football brands are also surrounded by a broader network of more than averagely "involved" stakeholders. While a traditional brand may underperform and have customer complaints, these blips may pass undetected by the majority of customers, and do not have a major impact on the brand's standing.

Football brands are very much in the public eye. As well as the paying customers, the owners and directors of the club are often fans themselves, and are intensely involved in the club. Those who report on the club in the media, particularly local media, are also often fans, and are keen to know everything that is happening at the club. Advances in technology create 24/7 sports news channels and Internet sites hungry for stories about their favorite stars. For managers, every tactic that goes wrong, every aspect of team selection, every gesture on the touchline, will be replayed and analyzed in the media. Football is the ultimate results-driven business, where the average tenure of a manager is less than

18 months, and almost 50 percent of all first-time managers never get another job. The pressures on football brands also far outstrip those facing brands in other categories.

Structure of the book

Given the unique nature of football brands and the challenges facing those who manage them, this book first explores the nature of the football brands (Chapter 1) and the relationships between them and fans (Chapter 2) and other stakeholders (Chapter 3). It then goes on to explore some of the distinctive challenges facing football brands as service experiences (Chapter 4), in the light of global interest in football (Chapter 5) and throughout their lifecycle (Chapter 6).

Chapter 1 begins with an analysis of what makes a football brand. Chapter 2 explores the characteristics of brands, both those that are externally visible – such as logo and name – and those that lie below the surface, such as the values they represent, the organizational culture, which must be consistent with these values, and the brand's positioning and its personality. These are explained in relation to all brands, then each aspect in turn is discussed in relation to football.

Chapter 3 discusses brand equity, or what a brand is worth. It reviews the different methods of measurement that are proposed by marketing literature. These range from financial estimation of the value of a brand, through to frameworks to assess the dimensions of a brand that appeal to customers. The different approaches are considered in the marketing of all brands, then specifically for football brands. Once the book has explored the most successful football brands and the foundations on which these are based, Chapter 3 then looks at how fans engage with these brands.

Some fans will be highly involved with a football brand. These "highly identified" fans are of great interest as they are most likely to attend matches, become involved in club activities, and have a strong emotional attachment to the club. Not all fans will have this level of identification. Other fans may go to matches with family and friends, but see this as more of a social activity, and do not develop the same level of emotional attachment. Various frameworks have identified different types of fans and analyzed their identification with a football brand, and what they want from supporting it.

In Chapter 3, the context surrounding football brands is explored more fully. Different stakeholders are identified who play a role in the success of football brands. These include owners, media, and individual players. Some of the key issues in understanding each of these are explained in turn. The chapter also explores football communities and the role that they play for fans.

Services and branding literature increasingly focuses upon the whole experience that a customer has when they come into contact with the brand. Brand experiences and service experiences are particularly applicable to sports, where experiences can be designed to engage effectively with fans. Stadia are ideal venues for the use of color, multimedia, and different types of experience alongside the live sport event to build loyalty in fans. Chapter 4 explores the lessons from brand experiences and services marketing for football brands.

The global nature of football and differences in how fans support and relate to football brands are explored in Chapter 5. Once we have looked at drivers of globalization and the implications of these for marketing, Chapter 5 then considers whether football is a global game, looks at different patterns of consumption of the game, and also considers the new virtual communities of fans who have built up around clubs.

The book concludes with Chapter 6, which looks at the challenges of maintaining and building success in football brands given the strong link between on-the-pitch success and brand performance. Different contexts of clubs that are building success, revitalizing, or even rebuilding brands are contrasted with those in which marketers are tasked with maintaining the success of leading global football brands.

CHAPTER 1

What is a football brand?

Characteristics of brands

Davidson (1998) describes the brand as an iceberg. This is a useful analogy as only a small proportion of an iceberg is visible above the surface, and many other aspects are below the waterline. A brand tends to have a visible logo (a sign associated with the brand) and name, but may have other aspects, such as the values and culture that underpin these.

This chapter begins with a brief review of the different components of a brand, then goes on to discuss how these relate to football brands.

External

Logo

The American Marketing Academy (AMA) in 1960 defined a brand as "A name, term, sign, symbol or design, or a combination of them, intended to identify the goods of services of one seller or group of sellers and to differentiate them from those of competitors."

This definition highlights the importance to branding of the externally visible elements of the "iceberg" such as the logo and name. From McDonald's Golden Arches to Nike's Swoosh, these symbols of the brand are particularly valuable as brands become global. Without using words, if the brand has strong awareness with customers, a plethora of values and associations will spring to a customer's mind when they see the particular symbol.

Name

What's in a name? Many of today's leading brands are actually "legacy brands" whose names are those of the original founders of the company behind the brand, such as Levi Strauss, Heinz, and McDonald's. Other, and often more recent, brands have manufactured names which have been created to reflect the values of a brand. Examples of this include First Direct, the UK telephone and Internet banking division of HSBC, and Orange mobile phones, whose names were created especially for these companies and their offer to customers. These may have a particular meaning that fits with the product or service, such as iTunes or lastminute. com, which pretty well describe what the company does. Others are onomatopoeic: that is, they reflect a noise that fits with the product. Examples of this phenomenon are Wisk washing powder and Cillit Bang cleaning products. Alternatively names might be designed to be memorable. The Sony brand name was introduced in 1958, as the Japanese firm became more successful in selling its products globally. The Sony website explains the brand name as deriving from *Sonus,* the Latin word for sonic or sound, and "sonny", denoting small size, or a youth. The name was chosen because of its simple pronunciation in any language (http://www.sony.net/SonyInfo/CorporateInfo/History/index.html).

Internal

Core values

The internal identity of a brand comprises the core values of the organization. These are the foundation of a brand. Successful brands can clearly identify, and communicate to others, what these values are. If a brand is not authentic – for example, the brand communication emphasizes excellent customer service, but the organization does not believe in and behave in ways consistent with this excellence – customers will soon become cynical about the brand. People are now inundated with marketing messages from all different kinds of organizations, and have become much more adept at filtering information to pick out what represents real values and what does not.

The core values should be simple, credible, and justifiable.

If a car brand is based on engineering excellence, a customer will expect evidence of this excellence in performance, driving experience, and so on. Some values are less tangible and more emotional: these might for example relate to the trustworthiness, tradition, or community spirit of the brand. A customer would still, however, expect the organization behind the brand to behave in ways consistent with these values, and be trustworthy, mindful of traditional values, or make a contribution to the community.

According to Millward Brown in 2009, Google is the world's most valuable brand. A simple search on the Internet reveals ten clearly stated corporate values that underlie the Google brand. These are:

1 Focus on the user and all else will follow.
2 It's best to do one thing really, really well.
3 Fast is better than slow.
4 Democracy on the web works.
5 You don't need to be at your desk to need an answer.
6 You can make money without doing evil.
7 There's always more information out there.
8 The need for information crosses all borders.
9 You can be serious without a suit.
10 Great just isn't good enough.
        (Google 10 things: http://www.google.com/corporate/
                                        tenthings.html)

Core values are those that are so much a part of the brand and the company behind it that the company would not exist in the same form if they were not there. A company might outsource production, and buy in IT support, but have certain things that it can do better than anyone else, or that others cannot do in nearly the same way. Note that these core values must be values that customers perceive as benefits, be distinctive, and be sustainable, to support a successful brand. At the height of the dot.com boom many entrepreneurs would get carried away with the potential of the Internet as a channel, talk at length about how many clicks the website was getting, how extensive a database of potential customer contacts they had, and how global the potential market was, without recognizing the fact that only dot.com companies offering value and a distinctive ability would thrive in the market. Many "me too" companies fell by the wayside regardless of the technological possibilities.

Positioning

In strategic terms, a brand may be designed to fit with the perceived values of a customer. Lidl and Aldi supermarkets are positioned at the value, low-price, and limited range end of the spectrum of supermarket brands. Carrefour, Wal-Mart, and Costco are seen as hypermarkets which offer low prices across an extended range of product areas, whereas Waitrose, Tesco, and Marks & Spencer are perceived to be at the quality end of the spectrum of brand positioning.

Organizations should note a number of important considerations of brand positioning. First, this should be the perception of customers, not just the organization. Ries and Trout (1986) emphasize the need for positioning to be based on "what happens in the customer's mind." Organizations should research how their brands are perceived to check that there is not a gap between organizational and customer perceptions. Second, the positioning must be based on one or more real values offered by the brand, which will be communicated to customers, and which will allow them to understand the brand compared with its competitors. Finally, these values should be important to the customer. Organizations sometimes wrongly identify product or service features as values, when these are not seen as benefits by customers.

Culture

An organization's staff must then "live" the values of the brand for these to come across effectively to customers. Definitions of organizational culture, such as that of Johnson and Scholes (1992) identify dimensions of culture. Johnson and Scholes focus on six dimensions of culture:

- stories
- rituals and routines
- symbols
- organizational structure

- control systems
- power structures.

So, for example, subsidiaries of the Virgin brand have flat structures designed to encourage ideas and participation of all levels of staff in developing and improving brands and service offerings. An organization may have particular ways of behaving. For example, Warwick Business School has coffee in the lounge at 10.30 every morning. Staff know that it is possible to catch up and have a relaxed conversation with others at this time, and often choose to do this if they only need a quick word, rather than arranging a more formal conversation. Many ideas, research bids, and other joint initiatives have begun this way. An organization may also use its own terminology, have its own ways of working, and use anchor words or symbols which act as shorthand for more complex ideas.

Personality

Aaker (1997) talks about brands in terms of personalities. Hence Raid insect spray might be associated with a "tough" type of individual. The can of insecticide is often shown striding around in adverts as though it were an actual person. In other cases, a brand has been attributed with other human values such as "friendly," "accessible," or "youthful." These more emotional associations with brands are particularly useful to organizations now that technology makes it easier to replicate the functional and rational capabilities of competitors. Emotional values might be linked to the use of celebrities, or be symbolized in the design or the product or service, where and how it is sold. For 30 years, Absolut Vodka differentiated itself by its iconic shape of its bottle. Now it focuses on living in an "Absolut world," and describes this world as having the values of witty, creative, inspiring, interesting, and challenging the status quo (http://www.absolut.com/uk/about/story).

What are football brands?

As discussed in the introduction to this book, any of the following might be considered to be a football brand:

- a football club
- a football player
- a national football team
- a football body
- a football competition or tournament.

This book talks predominantly about the first of these, but in some chapters, such as Chapter 3, and in its use of practical football brand cases, it also focuses on the other types of football brand.

In Chapter 3 discussion revolves around the challenges of image for individual football stars, and the insights that can be gained from taking a marketing perspective to managing and marketing these images. In Chapter 5, one of the examples used for internationalization of football brands is the perceptions that Chinese fans had of the England national football team brand in the run-up to the Germany 2006 World Cup. This is contrasted with perceptions of other national brands. The book also discusses the development of football bodies, such as the League Managers Association, which have developed into brands in their own right, and the branding of bids to host football competitions, such as the FIFA World Cup, through the case of Sunderland's 2018/2022 World Cup bid.

How do the attributes of brands identified above apply to football brands?

External

Logo

Many football clubs have as their logo a badge traditionally associated with the football club. As with many other brand logos, such as McDonald's Golden Arches or the Nike Swoosh, many football fans would be able to identify badges such as that of Manchester United even if the name of the club were obscured.

In how many cases, though, do fans, even of that club, know the symbolism that lies behind the logos? A number of football clubs have had different badges or crests over time, and may have changed them to reflect altered circumstances, different stadia, and so on. My own club, Sunderland AFC, had the following badge from 1977–97, during the years in which I first supported the club:

Figure 1.1 Sunderland AFC badge 1977–97

In 1997, however, the club unveiled a new club crest to coincide with the move from Roker Park to the Stadium of Light. The new crest comprises images of landmarks, such as Wearmouth Bridge and Penshaw Monument, with a colliery wheel to reflect both mining tradition and the fact that the new stadium is built on the site of a former coal mine. The club explains that the new crest is designed to pay tribute to the club's fans across the region, and includes images from different parts of the area from which fans come.

Figure 1.2 New Sunderland AFC badge

The Sunderland AFC crest that I remember was only used from 1977 to 1997, and was based on, but not identical to, the badge that was used prior to this time. In fact, on its formation in 1884, Sunderland did not play in red and white at all, but in an all-blue strip until the 1887–88 season. The older badges included a ship to reflect the heritage of Sunderland in shipbuilding, the upper part of the Sunderland heraldic crest, and a lucky black cat. This was simplified to a ship, football, and red and white stripes in the 1977 version.

Similarly, a number of other football clubs have changed their crest, or logo, over the years. Fulham FC explains a transition from its earliest badge, which was a black and white representation of its ground, Craven Cottage, to the crest of the London Borough of Hammersmith, used from 1947, to a "retro" Fulham FC logo, a reversion to the London Borough of Hammersmith logo, and finally, in 2001, based on research which showed that only 14 percent of the club's fans recognized this logo (http://www.footballcrests.com/clubs/fulham-fc), to a simplified version of the club's initials.

Everton FC attributes the origins of its club crest to the club secretary, Theo Kelly, at the end of the 1937–38 season. This gentleman later became the club's manager. He wished to create a club tie, had agreement that this should be blue, but did not have a crest to put on the tie. Eventually he decided on the tower, or beacon, a building that stands at the heart of the area (built in 1787, this tower, originally built as a prison, still stands on Everton Brow). Laurels have the heraldic meaning of "winners," and laurel wreaths are still given to successful athletes, such as Olympians and Formula One drivers. The crest continues to this day.

Real Madrid originally had a crest that showed its initials (MFC – Madrid Club de Fútbal), but streamlined this inside a circle in 1908, and altered it again in 1920 when King Alfonso III granted the club his royal patronage, and the club's name changed to Real Madrid. On abolition of the monarchy in 1931, both the crown and the title of "Real" were removed from the club. The crown was replaced by a mulberry stripe to signify the region of Castile. The crown and title of Real were reinstated in 1941, but the mulberry stripe was also retained. In 2001 the club streamlined its badge, and the mulberry stripe took on more of a blue color.

Manchester United's crest is based on that of the City of Manchester. It has been through a number of versions but has retained the same basic shape. The devil on the central badge derives from the club's nickname of "Red Devils," which was adopted in the early 1960s. This was incorporated into the club badge in 1970.

FC Bayern Munich (Fußball-Club Bayern München), Germany's most successful and well-known football team, has had a number of different crests. Originally the crest was a stylized version of the initials FCBM interwoven. In 1951 the central blue and white section – which is the flag of the Bavarian (Bayerisch) region – was incorporated.

As can be seen by this brief consideration of a very small number of football clubs, this book could be filled entirely by discussion of how different football clubs' crests evolved and the reason behind the changes that have been made. Given constraints on word length, a full discussion of this topic and descriptions of the history of a large number of football crests can be found at the excellent <http://www.footballcrests.com/index.php>.

For the purposes of this discussion, the following conclusions are drawn:

- Club logos are based largely on historical club crests. Some of these have been redrawn – and often simplified – in relatively recent times. A number of clubs explicitly identify this as being in recognition of the fact that these crests have become logos.
- Many club logos incorporate the club's initials.
- Regional heraldic crests often feature.
- Colors are significant, with logos often heavily featuring the color of the club's shirt colors, often in conjunction with colors that have regional or other significance.
- Local buildings and landmarks also feature frequently on football club logos, suggesting the importance of local and regional values.
- The club's lucky mascot often features on the logo.
- Some clubs have a long history of including the badge or logo on the club's football shirts. Again, this is sometimes a relatively recent development.

It should be remembered that modern football shirts differ in a number of ways from older football shirts. The Football League Management Committee decreed that football players should wear numbers of the back of their shirts in 1939. Conventions on which player wore which number changed over the years until the 1954 World Cup, when FIFA introduced squad numbering. Individual numbers became less significant but a player would wear the same number throughout, even if he played in a different position. The first time player names were included on shirts in England alongside squad numbers was as recent as the League Cup Final in 1993. The use of names was then expanded to the English Premier League in 1993–94, and shirts with player names were first used in the 1994 World Cup Tournament in the United States. Introduction of names and numbers on club shirts greatly expanded the market for replica shirts.

Name

A number of different conventions apply to football club names. Most typically, the name is that of the town or city, followed by a word to signify the unity of the club, and FC for football club. Typical examples are Newcastle United, Bradford City, and West Bromwich Albion.

Among current English Football League clubs, 26 clubs simply have the name of the place followed by Football Club or Association Football Club. The most common second part of a football club name in England is United (14 clubs), then City (13 clubs), and Town (10 clubs). There are four clubs that use Albion, four Rovers, three County, three Athletic, three Wanderers, and one each of Alexandra, Rangers, Forest, Hotspur, Argyle, Wednesday, North End, Orient, Stanley, Villa, and Dons. The full list is given in Table 1.1.

While some of the names are self-explanatory, such as City, Town, County, and Athletic, others merit a little discussion, and had historical or specific meaning:

- The *Wanderers* name may go back to the Wanderers Football Club, an amateur team based in Battersea, London in the 1860s and 1870s. This club won the first-ever Football Association Cup in 1872, and won the competition four more times throughout the 1870s. Such was the reputation of the club that it may well have influenced the names of other football clubs that adopted the tag "Wanderers."

Table 1.1 Names of English football clubs

Name only	United	City
Arsenal	Manchester	Birmingham
Chelsea	West Ham	Hull
Fulham	Newcastle	Manchester
Liverpool	Peterborough	Stoke
Sunderland	Scunthorpe	Bristol
Burnley	Sheffield	Cardiff
Everton	Colchester	Coventry
Portsmouth	Southend	Swansea
Barnsley	Carlisle	Leicester
Blackpool	Hartlepool	Norwich
Crystal Palace	Leeds	Bradford
Middlesbrough	Hereford	Exeter
Reading	Rotherham	Lincoln
Watford	Torquay	
Brentford		**Albion**
Gillingham	**Town**	West Bromwich
Millwall	Ipswich	Brighton and Hove
Southampton	Huddersfield	Burton
Walsall	Yeovil	
Barnet	Aldershot	**Athletic**
Chesterfield	Cheltenham	Wigan
Dagenham and Redbridge	Shrewsbury	Charlton
Darlington	Grimsby	Oldham
Morecambe	Macclesfield	
Port Vale	Northampton	**County**
Rochdale		Derby
	Wanderers	Stockport
Rovers	Bolton	Notts
Blackburn	Wolverhampton	
Doncaster	Wycombe	
Bristol		
Tranmere		
Crewe Alexandra	Plymouth Argyle	Sheffield Wednesday
Queens Park Rangers	Leyton Orient	Preston North End
Tottenham Hotspur	Accrington Stanley	Aston Villa
Nottingham Forest	Milton Keynes Dons	

- *Albion* is the oldest known name of the island of Great Britain, and seems to refer to the British roots of the clubs.
- The precise meaning of *Rovers* is not clear, but this is assumed to relate to clubs traveling around, and have similar roots to Wanderers.

- Plymouth Argyle Football Club was originally called Argyle Football Club. The origins of the name *Argyle* are not clear, with this being attributed either to Argyle Street where the committee met, or because the founders may have admired the football skills of the Argyle and Sutherland Highlanders, then based in the area.
- The Crewe *Alexandra* name is attributed by the club to Princess Alexandra, although it has also been suggested that the name might refer to a pub in which the original committee held their meetings.
- The Accrington *Stanley* name arose when the original Accrington Football Club (one of 12 founder members of the Football League in 1888) folded because of financial problems and was replaced by a team called Stanley Villa, named after the street in which it was based. (http://www.accringtonobserver. co.uk/news/s/48/48015_the_worlds_most_famous_club.html). The Stanley team took on the name of Accrington Stanley on the demise of Accrington FC, presumably to gain its place in the Football League.
- The Nottingham *Forest* name – and the logo with a tree on it – do not come from nearby Sherwood Forest, but from the Forest Recreation Ground where the club first played on its formation in 1865.
- Sheffield *Wednesday* was, until 1929, known as the Wednesday Football Club. It took its name from the Wednesday cricket club, which played its matches on this day. The football team was formed to keep the cricket players fit during winter. Indeed, until relatively recent times it was not uncommon for professional sportsmen to play cricket in summer and football in winter. Famous examples of this were Arthur Milton and Denis Compton.
- The name Tottenham *Hotspur* is based on a 14th-century knight, Sir Henry Percy, who was known as Harry Hotspur and owned land around the Tottenham area. Sir Henry was renowned for his warrior spirit and embodied a set of fighting qualities that the club saw as symbolizing its spirit. The club's motto is *Audere est Facere* (to dare is to do).
- The *United* tag has symbolic meanings of togetherness and team spirit, and has been adopted by a number of teams.

International football club names

Most commonly football clubs in other countries follow a similar pattern, in that they use a place name followed by Football Club, or Sporting Club in the language of the country. Hence football clubs are often FC (Fussball Club) or SV (Sporting Verein) in Germany. VfL, as in VfL Osnabrück, stands for Verein für Leibesübung (club for exercise of the body). More detail of international football club names and origins is given below:

- **Bundesliga in Germany**: *Eintracht*, as in Eintracht Frankfurt, Eintracht Braunschweig, and Eintracht Schalke, is the equivalent of unity. *Borussia,* as in Borussia Dortmund and Borussia Mönchengladbach, is Latin for Prussia, the area now known as Nord-Rhein-Westfalia. Borussia Dortmund is said to have been named after the nearby Borussia brewery.
- **La Liga in Spain:** Other tags include self-explanatory names such as Sporting alongside:
  - *Real,* as in Real Madrid, Real Betis, Real Mallorca, and Real Racing Club de Santander, denotes the award of royal patronage to the club.
  - *Deportivo,* as in Deportivo de Coruna, means sporting. Hence Deportivo de Coruna, whose full name is Real Club Deportivo de La Coruña, S.A.D. (in English Royal Sports Club of La Coruna), but the prefix is also used in Deportivo Getafe, Deportivo Espanyol, and even the Peruvian Deportivo Wanka. Officials at the latter club reported themselves bemused at a sudden rush of orders from English-speaking countries for their team shirts (http://www.thesun.co.uk/sol/homepage/news/article36882.ece). See Chapter 5 for issues in globalization of football brands.
- **La Ligue, now Ligue 1 in France:** In the French leagues, *AS* (as in AS Monaco, AS Nancy, AS Saint-Etienne) stands for Association Sportive. Another commonly used prefix is *Olympique,* as in Olympique Lyonnais, Olympique de Marseilles, and Olympique Gymnaste Club de Nice-Côte d'Azur, known as OGC Nice or simply Nice. The use of Olympic in football club names is also found in Greece, with Olympiacos Sports Club of Piraeus, often known as Olympiakos, and Olympiakos

Nicosia in Cyprus. The word Olympic, best known for its use in the Olympic Games, refers to Mount Olympus in Greece. In ancient Greece, this was regarded as the abode of the gods, where Zeus had his throne.

- **Eredivisie in the Netherlands:** *PSV,* as in PSV Eindhoven, refers to Philips Sporting Vereniging (Philips Sporting Union), as the Philips Corporation has its headquarters in Eindhoven and PSV began as a works team for Philips employees. Possibly the longest football club name is that of *NAC* Breda in the Dutch Eredivisie (First Division). NAC Breda, often known as NAC, was founded in 1912 with the combination of two clubs, ADVENDO and NOAD. NOAD stood for Nooit Opgeven, Altijd Doorzetten (English: never give up, always persevere). ADVENDO stands for Aangenaam Door Vermaak En Nuttig Door Ontspanning Combinatie (English: pleasant for entertainment and useful for relaxation). Hence the full name of NAC is Nooit opgeven altijd doorzetten, Aangenaam door vermaak en nuttig door ontspanning, Combinatie. This is abbreviated to Nooit Aangenaam Combinatie (can that really mean the "never pleasant club?"). Breda was added to thank the City of Breda for buying the club's stadium when the club got into financial problems in 2003!

Brand values

Corporate brands

It should be noted that in football, brands are corporate brands. No organization is allowed by league rules to own more than one football club, so in football terms the organization owns only one club or brand with which it is inherently linked.

There are, however, two arguments that suggest football brands might not remain as corporate brands.

First, there has been a recent trend towards combined ownership of a football club with another type of sporting club, which might result in conglomerates which own several sports brands. For example, until recently one organization owned Wycombe Wanderers Football Club (of the English Football League) and Wasps Rugby Union team (of the Zurich Premier League).

Manchester United Football Club (English Premier League) and the American Football (NFL) team, the Tampa Bay Buccaneers, are both owned by Malcolm Glazer. Likewise, Randy Lerner owns Cleveland Browns (NFL) and Aston Villa Football Club (English Premier League). For now, however, football brands are considered to be corporate brands.

Second, a number of football brands have changed owners frequently in recent years. Financial difficulties at one end of the league structure, and the potential to expand globally attractive brands at the other, have resulted in an unprecedented number of takeovers of football clubs. The amounts of money required to buy a football club, in particular an English Premier League club, mean that buying a larger football club is now the preserve of multi-millionaires or even billionaires, rather than the wealthy local businessmen of even a decade ago. In several instances, it would appear that the football club is bought for the potential of its brand. Football clubs in the English Premier League, La Liga, Serie A, and other successful football leagues have global reach – because of global broadcasting deals. They have high awareness, as fans on a global scale become interested in both the football they play and the high-profile celebrity players and the actress/popstar girlfriends with whom they are often associated. They have a large potential fan base. Football is a global sport, and several large markets, such as China, India, and the United States, remain relatively untapped.

For now, however, we might consider football brands as corporate brands in which the organization plays a prominent role and "stands behind the offering that the customer buys or uses" (Aaker 2004). The corporate values dominate any branding strategy. This is certainly still true for a majority of football brands, and makes it vitally important that the employees of the football clubs are guided in their behavior towards fans and other stakeholders by the values associated with the brand.

Dual aims

Any sporting player, club, or body has sporting aims. As the game of football has developed from being a beautiful game into a multi-billion-pound global business, football has also developed a set of commercial imperatives. While the joy of the game may still motivate a player, players change hands for significant sums of money. At the top tier of the game they earn large sums of money, and therefore, sensibly, players and those that represent them will also develop an understanding of the player's value and the value of the player's brand. Commercial contracts often contain agreed sums that a player will be paid in "image rights" for the use of their name and image (that is, their "brand") in the marketing of the club. Similarly, football bodies are often representative of a set of members, for example the Professional Footballers' Association or League Managers Association, but have to balance the books and generate sufficient revenue to meet the needs of their members or "customers." In other instances, the football body may be an overarching organization. Hence the Premier League, Football League, Serie A, or J League (Japan) has a set of clubs, fans, and other stakeholders whose needs they serve and represent in a given season. The different types of football brands all have some degree of commercial aims alongside their sporting ambitions.

The extent of control over the commercial aspects of football varies by country. So, for example, football player wages are capped in Germany's top league, the Bundesliga, and the maximum percentage of player wages to revenue is capped at 60 percent in the English Football League. Revenue is distributed equally among member clubs of the MLS (Major League Soccer) in the United States, but a free market determines the level of player wages in many other football leagues.

Football leagues work differently, depending on their constitution and the rules that they have evolved. So, for example, the MLS in the United States has a set of members that cannot be promoted or relegated. To maintain competitive balance, revenue and star players are shared out among clubs to make sure that there is relatively even competition among clubs in the league. In England, the Premier League, the world's richest football league, represents its member clubs in collective bargaining for television broadcast rights, and broadcasting money is then allocated to clubs on a sliding scale depending where in the league the club finished in the previous season. In Spanish La Liga, however, clubs negotiate their own broadcasting deals.

The main focus of this book is upon football clubs as brands. It must be remembered that even the largest and most successful football clubs are the equivalent of small businesses. Successful clubs, such as Manchester United, Real Madrid, Inter Milan, and Bayern München, have, however, built very successful global brands. Such are the awareness levels, and comments such as "Manchester United, a global brand as familiar as Coca-Cola" are not uncommon. While in some respects this is true, we must bear in mind the massive difference in the revenues and operating profits of multinational corporations and football clubs. Even the most globally successful football clubs, such as Manchester United, are nearer to the revenue and number of employees of a small or medium-sized enterprise than a multinational corporation.

Football brands are managed by organizations on a dramatically different scale from other highly visible global brands. Their boards and directors must also manage the potential trade-off between sporting and commercial aims.

Perceived values

During a study for the Football Association into how Chinese fans perceived the national football brands of other countries in the run-up to the 2006 World Cup (Bridgewater 2004), fans were asked to provide words that they associated with each of a number of national teams. The main responses – where these were repeatable – are listed in Table 1.2.

When grouped into categories, a number of themes emerged. These are shown in Figure 1.3.

The frequent references to color are perhaps surprising. These relate to the color of football strips and this is a visual image, which may be noticeable in televised coverage. This may in itself be significant for teams such as England, which changes from red to white strips in different matches, and did not have a strong color association among fans. Italy, France, and Holland all had strong perceived associations with the color of their football strips, but all have strikingly colored football strips. Awareness of recent performance is also not too surprising, nor perhaps is an awareness of the stars belonging to particular teams. It was,

Table 1.2 How Chinese fans perceive national football brands

	How many positive	How many negative	Total	Key words
Germany	162	17	179	Tank, solid, strong, discipline, effective
Brazil	193	11	204	Samba, dance, passion, skill, lazy
France	125	12	137	Zidane, blue, old
Italy	124	35	159	Blue, handsome, defence, cheat
Argentina	123	17	140	Maradona, skill, passion, cheat
Spain	84	25	109	Bull, Raul, underachieve
Japan	21	35	56	Hardworker, rising, short
England	157	53	210	Beckham, stars, handsome, disappointing
Holland	88	20	108	Orange, total football, aggressive
Portugal	68	20	88	Figo, dark (black) horse, skilful, divers.

Color	Holland – orange, Italy – blue, France – blue
Performance	England –disappointing, Portugal – improving, unexpected (in World Cup 2006), Spain – lose important games
Stars	France – Zidane, Henry, England – Beckham, Italy – Totti, Holland – Van Basten, Portugal – Figo, Cristiano Ronaldo
Style of play	Brazil – samba, dance, Germany – solid, rigid, Italy – defensive, Holland – total football
National symbol	Holland – tulip, Germany – iron, Spain – bull, Japan – cherry blossom

Figure 1.3 Main themes associated with international teams

however, surprising how far back recall of players went. Chinese football fans made several references to Bobby Charlton even though a majority of the respondents were not born in 1966, the year of his greatest success. Respondents also referred to wives and girlfriends, particularly of England players, and explained in focus groups that this is because these celebrities make it onto the front pages, as well as the sports pages, of newspapers and magazines. This may be a more likely association of occasional or even non-fans rather than of fervent football fans.

The most interesting values that fans perceived as important in football brands concerned the team's style of play. This could be positive or negative, but was often portrayed positively. Germany was more often praised for being solid than criticized for being rigid. Brazil had a very high positive score based on its samba style, although interestingly it did not rank highest in awareness among Chinese fans. England had the highest awareness ranking, probably for the reasons explained above, and the extensive televised coverage of English Premier League matches.

Quite often stereotypical symbols associated with a country were also given, such as Japan "cherry blossom" or Spain "bull."

Brand values of Premier League football clubs

In 2002, a study by Bridgewater and Stray into what mattered to over 3,500 fans during the 2000–01 season identified five "factors" or dimensions. These were:

Organizational values

Fans were concerned that the clubs that they supported were financially stable. They wanted their clubs to have funds either to build upon or to achieve greater success, and to plan for future growth. Stable and "good" management of clubs was also considered important. Fans wanted to see a strong youth academy, an effective manager and coaches, and a go-ahead board of directors. Ethics and community relations were also considered important. Fans value honesty and integrity in the club they support, and it matters to them that the club has a good relationship with the community.

Team support

Fans were very concerned about whether a team was "perceived" to be successful by themselves, and also by fans of rival clubs.

If a club was perceived to be successful, the fan engaged in a set of activities connected with the club. These went beyond attending matches to talking about the team, attending club events, buying merchandise, going into club-related web boards, and becoming more interested in football as a whole. The perception that a team was doing well was not always about actual performance. For example, in 2000–01, the team perceived by their fans to be doing best was newly promoted Ipswich Town, which had far exceeded the expectations of its fans with a fifth-place finish. Manchester United was ranked as having achieved "about what was expected," even though it won the Premier League. This was a reflection of the team winning the treble (the Premier League, Champions League, and FA Cup) two seasons before, which had raised the expectation levels of fans to such a degree that success in the domestic league alone was not considered very significant. Conversely fans distance themselves from these activities if they perceive the team is not doing well.

History, symbols, and perceived knowledge

Football has a considerable history. Many clubs around the world are well over 100 years old. As described earlier, football brands have lengthy traditions, and may also have strong family and regional associations. Fans often placed a value on the tradition, the team logo, motto, sponsors, the mascot, and the nickname. They had extensive knowledge of classic victories, goal scorers and opponents in cup runs, and other past successes. The emotional value placed on these "symbols" associated with football brands may explain why fans can sometimes respond negatively to proposed relocation, changes to club logo, team strip, or even stadium name.

Social activities

Football brands have a social dimension. Involvement in supporting a club may mean going to matches with friends, meeting a social group before and after matches, using official transport, and knowing the people who sit next to you in a stadium. One fan explained how he had sat next to more than one generation of the family who hold the season tickets next to him at his club. Increasingly this social dimension may extend to virtual, or web-based, communities. Although some of those on the web boards may never have physically met those with whom they communicate, strong social support links are forged such that fans have been known to group together to pay for a fellow fan to come to a match, or have supported fellow fans through personal problems, and even supported terminally ill fans in their last days.

Self-esteem

There is an individual emotional attachment to football brands. Fans feel personally affected by success and failure. Respondents described an effect on their overall mood, how they would not want to go out socially, or even talk to family and friends if the team lost. This was made worse if the social activity would mean encountering fans of rival clubs who might rub in this failure. Conversely, if the team won, fans would want to talk to people about the team, the club, and reported feeling better about themselves.

Culture

As many football clubs are corporate brands, the dimensions of culture identified by Johnson and Scholes (1992) are particularly significant.

Stories

Support patterns in football are often parent to child, older member of the community to the rising generation of supporters. This is particularly the case for locally based football brands, where fans of a club may work and live together as well as supporting their local team. Even for football clubs with a globally dispersed fan base, however, the rise of the Internet makes it possible for fans to share stories of past glories and disasters irrespective of where they are based or what the time zone is.

How many fans of the England national team, who were alive

in 1966, can tell you where they were when England won the World Cup? How many fans can recount the exact detail of who played, who scored, a fantastic save, a shot missed, in a memorable match for their chosen club? Such stories bring to life the values of a football brand and are second best to being there for new fans.

Rituals and routines

Many aspects of football are surrounded by ritual and routine. Talk to players and they will tell stories of which boot they put on first, lucky socks, jumping in the air a certain number of times in the warm-up, or other ways in which they behave before every match because this has been lucky for them in the past. In the same way, the Everton secretary who developed the club logo (see page 18) spread the use of the logo because the team was successful in the games when officials wore the club ties which featured it. Football clubs in general have particular ways of behaving. In contrast to many other organizations, football club boardrooms and directors' boxes on match days are still very formal. Men must wear ties to be admitted, and special permission even has to be gained by the one or two club owners and chairmen, such as Mike Ashley at Newcastle United and Darragh MacAnthony at Peterborough United, who prefer not to wear ties.

While particular rituals and routines may seen strange when explained to others, each club will have its own way of behaving with staff and fans, and its own unwritten rules and behavior. These not only affect staff working for the club, but may influence the fans' experience of a game. For example all the corporate catering menus at Norwich City were selected by major shareholder Delia Smith, a renowned chef. Many new stadia have excellent members' bars with memorabilia from famous victories and efficient catering, whereas older stadia are sometimes quirky but retain an atmosphere and tradition which many feel is lacking in more modern, purpose-built stadia. Many of the famous stands built by Archibald Leach have gone with the move to modern stadia, but a few remain, such as that at Everton's Goodison Park.

Rituals and routines may surround how fans buy tickets, how

and with whom they travel to home and away matches, and which seat they sit in. There are instances of outrage where fans are asked to move to a different seat for their season ticket. In 1999, when Newcastle United asked bond holders, who had purchased their tickets for ten years, to move to different seats so that it could incorporate more space for corporate hospitality, fans mounted a "Save our Seats" campaign, and some fans took the club to the High Court. Similarly, when fans are told about moves to new stadia, which may make economic sense, the club often underestimates the unwritten rules that it must abide by. For example, when Everton fans were told of a proposed move to relocate the football ground to Kirby, which is outside the Liverpool city boundary, a 60 percent majority of fans voted yes in a ballot, but 11,000 fans became involved in a "Keep Everton in our city" campaign, such was their strength of feeling about this tradition.

Symbols

There is an increasing awareness in football about the importance of the club's badge or logo, and a number of clubs have streamlined these so that they are clear, are used consistently in marketing communication, and may even have changed them to be appropriate to the modern-day values of the club. A number of other symbols are also associated with football brands.

On some occasions when clubs have proposed to change a club's logo, they find that fans have particular allegiance to an old version that they feel has emotional value. This is a challenge for all brands as they seek to evolve and remain relevant. There have been highly publicized episodes of this happening in other sectors. Coca-Cola, for example, changed to a new taste in 1985 and now describes this is a day "that will live in marketing infamy" (http://www.thecoca-colacompany.com/heritage/cokelore_newcoke.html), such was the outcry among consumers.

The taste variation may have appeared to Coca-Cola as a minor tweaking of the product behind the brand, but was seen as a step too far away from a brand which for its customers had emotional as well as rational values. Similarly, Kellogg's proposed a name change of Coco Pops cereal in the United Kingdom to Choco Crispies, to bring the brand names into line in different countries. Such was the backlash among UK customers at the loss of a familiar brand that the company soon changed the name back.

In football terms, some clubs have encountered problems with proposed changes to the club's logo. For example, in 2005, when Coventry City Football Club of the English Coca-Cola Football League Championship (second tier), proposed a new logo to mark the move from Highfield Road to the new Ricoh Arena, fans were not happy at the changes. Fans commented that it was good to mark this major event in the club's history, but the new logo did not feature the phoenix, which represented either Lady Godiva's husband Leofric, or perhaps alternatively the city being rebuilt from the flames following its major post-war reconstruction. The castle on top of the elephant had also been removed, as had the football. The club responded to fans' concerns by dropping the proposed changes and sticking to the previous club logo.

Organizational structure, control systems, and power structures

There are a number of different organizational structures in football. In some countries, the president of the club is elected. The world's richest football club, Real Madrid, has been owned and operated by its members (*Socios)* since its formation. The members elect a president to run the club. The longest-serving president was Santiago Bernabeu Yeste, who served from 1943–78. The new stadium built during his tenure was given his name in 1955 although it had been built in 1947.

In June 2009, Florentino Perez was elected the new president of Real Madrid Football Club. On this occasion there was no rival candidate, as three other candidates who had initially declared an intention to stand (Eugenio Martinez Bravo, Juan Onieva, and Eduardo Garcia) pulled out of the running, perhaps put off by the large (€57.4 million) guarantee asked of candidates. Previously, potential presidents of football clubs have run contested election campaigns similar to those in politics. They may win fans' votes by proposing to bring in a particular manager or players, or perhaps to dismiss a manager or sell existing players who are not popular with fans. Perez's first move was to remove Juande Ramos as manager and bring in Chilean coach Manuel Pellegrini.

Under this system, club presidents may return to a club. Perez was previously president of Real Madrid for a period between 2000 and 2006, and is considered "father of the *galácticos*" strategy, which saw the club bring in established successful but older players such as Luis Figo, David Beckham, Zinedine Zidane, and Ronaldo for large transfer fees. These players also attracted large numbers of fans to the club and were a boon for merchandise sales. Since the re-election of Perez, Brazilian playmaker Kaká has signed for Real Madrid for £56 million, a record transfer fee which was quickly surpassed with the signing of the Portuguese Cristiano Ronaldo from Manchester United for a massive £80 million transfer fee, seemingly a signal that Perez is assembling the *galácticos* II.

The system of elected presidents can also be seen in other Spanish clubs, for example FC Barcelona and Espanyol, where Daniel Sanchez Llibre has recently signaled his intent to stand down after nine years as president.

There are a number of different structures. Sometimes these vary across markets, but in some instances, such as England, different structures are adopted within the same market. Until 2007, for example, French football clubs were prohibited by French law from listing on the stock market, La Bourse. Many English clubs have now delisted from the London stock market (LSE), after finding that their shares did not retain their value and that the club might open itself up to hostile takeover bids. French clubs, however, saw European competitors seeming to benefit from a source of capital from which they were ruled out. Olympique Lyonnais became listed on the stock market in January 2007, the first French football club to do so. It was hoped that the funds raised would help Lyon with its ambitions to build a new 60,000 capacity stadium.

Within the English football game, between June 1996 and August 1997 after a major new broadcasting deal was announced, a number of clubs followed the example of Tottenham Hotspur in listing on the London stock market or on AIM (the Alternative Investment Market) or Ofex (Off-Exchange Investment). Many have since delisted, giving reasons such as the low liquidity of shares, the fall in value of shares, particularly in the current global economic downturn, and the unwillingness of corporate institutions to invest in football clubs. From the other side, investors have commented that, while there is money to be made particularly from the top end of football, this went more into player wages than to investors.

A majority of the clubs ended up worth a fraction of the original flotation price. Clubs in the United Kingdom who have listed shares include Arsenal (though not on the full market), Aberdeen (AIM), Aston Villa, Birmingham City, Bolton Wanderers (AIM), Bradford City, Celtic, Charlton Athletic, Chelsea (Village), Heart of Midlothian, Leeds United, Leicester City, Manchester United, Manchester City (Ofex), Millwall (Holdings), Newcastle United, Nottingham Forest, Preston North End, QPR, Rangers (Ofex), Sheffield United, Southampton (Leisure), Tottenham Hotspur, Watford (Leisure), and West Bromwich Albion (AIM). None of these still has a full market listing, although a small number still have AIM or junior market holdings. Stock market listing brought with it a set of reporting requirements. Companies that are listed on the London Stock Exchange agree to follow a set of codes on corporate governance, which provides guidelines for how they should run their businesses. These are designed to protect the assets of their businesses, and in turn the investment of the shareholders.

The dominant ownership structure in football in the United Kingdom is that of the private company, either a public limited company (PLC) or a limited company (Ltd). These structures do not have the same level of reporting requirements of listed companies, and may therefore be less costly for clubs to manage. The Combined Code on Corporate Governance does, however, make sensible recommendations designed to protect organizations, and its principles, such as an independent chairman and the role of independent non-executive directors, are still adopted by a number of clubs.

Some clubs are now opting for fan involvement in the running of football clubs. The cooperative model may involve a fan representative on the board, or a club that is run entirely by its supporters. These latter include Brentford and Exeter football clubs. Around 40 English league clubs have a Supporters Trust representative on their board.

How much involvement fans have in how their football club is run varies depending on the way the club is structured. Fans can feel disenfranchised if they do not agree with the way the club is being run and the decisions that are made. That said, they must be realistic about what is possible within the means of a club, but the more involvement fans have, the more they are likely to understand the reasons why particular decisions are made.

Brand personality

Because of the strong element of culture, tradition, and symbols associated with football brands, the attachment of fans is often highly emotional. The nature of this attachment and relationship with the brand are explored further in Chapter 2. It should be pointed out here, however, that different clubs adopt different strategies towards the individual celebrities who play for them.

We earlier discussed Real Madrid's *galácticos* strategy, whereby leading star players were brought to the club at great expense. These individual stars became the face of Real Madrid, and each might bring with him a dedicated fan base. So, for example, when David Beckham moved to Real Madrid from Manchester United, a majority of Manchester United fans continued to find the brand attractive, even if some part of its personality was diminished for them with the departure of a particular favorite. Other fans might identify so strongly with David Beckham, as a symbol of the brand of whichever club he plays for – Manchester United, Real Madrid, LA Galaxy, or AC Milan – that they switch their allegiance between these clubs as he moves on. Highly identified fans will now be throwing up their hands in horror at the very idea of such fickle support! This does, however, happen for a proportion of the fans, the customers of a football brand who are strongly attracted by a particular player. It is perhaps not surprising that when a new player, who may be an established star in his own country, joins a club, the fans and media of that country become interested in this club. When Junichi Inamoto moved to Arsenal in 2001, some Japanese fans and media became interested in the club. In fact, some reports at the time suggested that the Japanese fans were not all that swayed by this move, as Inamoto was a relatively low-profile player in Japan compared with Shinji Ono, who moved to Dutch club Feyenoord. Shinji Ono was seen as the real star in Japan at the time (http://news.bbc.co.uk/sport1/hi/ football/teams/a/arsenal/1454850.stm).

The idea that particular players bring with them a set of new supporters has also been seen with Greek player Stelios at Bolton, Turkish player Tugay at Blackburn Rovers, and more recently in 2005, South Korean player Ji-Sung Park at Manchester United.

The extent to which individual players play a role in the personality of football brands is considered further in Chapter 3.

Brand positioning

It is easy to assume that positioning of football brands is only a matter of the level at which the clubs play and of what aspirations they have and can afford. In fact, other aspects of brand also become important to fans, and may affect the way in which the brand is perceived in relation to its competitors. Whether implicitly or explicitly, some football brands are associated with a particular style of play: for example, the Brazil national team and "samba style," Holland and "total football." If the brand succeeds, but the football which is played does not match up to fan expectations, fans might still be disappointed at the performance.

Brand franchises

In US sports marketing, it is relatively common for the brand associated with a club to be referred to as a franchise. This "franchise" is awarded by the league – hence new franchises could be created by a league – and can be transferred between locations. The idea of a "golden share," the right to compete in a league, has recently been debated in football in the United Kingdom in the light of financial issues facing clubs – for example Leeds United, Luton, Rotherham, Bournemouth, and Chester City in England, and Livingston FC in Scotland. In each case, there was a discussion about whether the "golden share" would be awarded – and under what conditions – to new owners who took over these clubs.

The idea that a "right to play" might be separated from a particular location forms the basis of the idea of sports franchises. The franchise offers the right to play in a particular league under a particular and identifiable name. In 1996 there were 10 original franchises in Major League Soccer (MLS), but these will have expanded to 18 franchises by 2011. MLS officially announced that Portland, Oregon has been given the 18th franchise and will begin play in 2011, along with the fellow west coast city Vancouver, Canada. Two other franchises, Seattle Sounders and Philadelphia, commence in 2010 (for a fuller discussion of MLS, see Gary Hopkins' book *Star-Spangled Soccer*, 2010).

In the expansion phase, and without promotion or relegation issues to address, MLS has been able to expand the number of franchises it awards, and assesses cases for entry on the basis of location, facilities, and market. MLS proposed to admit more franchises and narrowed down contenders to seven final bids, from which it selected first Seattle and Philadelphia, then Portland and Vancouver. Unsuccessful bids included Miami, which previously operated in MLS for four years from 1998 as Miami Fusion, but drew poor attendances and ceased to operate after four seasons. The MLS and Miami-based businessman Marcelo Claure joined forces with FC Barcelona of Spain to assess the potential of reintroducing a franchise into the region, but this project foundered in the face of unfavorable market conditions. Montreal withdrew its bid, and Atlanta was not able to secure funding in time.

The elements that influence decisions of where to create franchises are location, tradition of soccer support, size of support, funding plans, and creation of stadia.

Once franchises are created, if they are unable to continue on the basis of any of these elements, franchisees have moved to different locations that are considered more favorable. For example, the San José Earthquakes in MLS moved to Houston at the end of the 2005 season, having failed to secure a soccer-specific stadium for the club. The owner, Anschutz Entertainment Group, took all of the players and played in Houston under the name Houston Dynamos. The "Earthquakes" name, one of the ten original franchises of MLS, was retained by the league for use with a future San José team and resumed operation in San José in 2008.

The concept of moving a football brand (because of changes in employment patterns or other economic and geographic circumstances in the original location) to a different location that may be better suited in the current era to support a football club, is relatively uncommon outside of the United States, although this did happen in the case of Wimbledon Football Club in England, which was relocated and renamed the MK (for Milton Keynes) Dons. This raises interesting questions about what lies at the heart of a football club and brand.

With sports franchises in the United States, the name becomes sufficiently well known and adds sufficient value that "buying" the brand is attractive to a new company even if that brand has to begin the process of building a club and attracting fans, rather than being part of a package with a stadium and fan base which is bought along with the brand.

DC United

If the rest of the world thinks of the United States and football at all, it will be either the Super Bowl (the glamour final of American football) or for soccer, soccer moms, whose glittering ranks include Victoria Beckham and Britney Spears, or as a girls' sport and something that is more about participation than spectators.

However, the average attendance at an MLS match (Forbes 2008) is 16,460, just short of that of the National Hockey League (17,147) and National Basketball Association (17,141), which people might consider as much bigger sports in the United States. Often the associations that people from outside the United States make with "soccer" are with Pelé, Rodney Marsh, and other European and Latin American footballers who were reaching the end of their playing careers, and made lifestyle moves to the United States in the 1970s.

The way in which MLS brands work is often confused. Sports brands are often referred to as franchises, and instances such as San José's move to Houston are discussed as examples of how these may be less geographically linked to particular cities or locations than in other football leagues. In fact, the valuable asset of these teams is the "right to play," or membership of the league. In English football leagues, this has come to be described as the "golden share," which does not automatically transfer to a new entity that might take over an existing club.

DC United, headquartered in Washington DC, is the most successful professional soccer organization in the history of the United States. They have been MLS Cup Champions four times – in 1996, 1997, 1999, and 2004 – and also won the 1996 US Open Cup, the 1998 CONCACAF Champions Cup, and the 1997, 1999, 2006, and 2007 MLS Supporters' Shields. Associated with star players such as Freddy Adu – a 14-year-old phenomenon when he became associated with DC United – the club is one of the more established names in the league. Indeed it has been referred to as the "Manchester United" of MLS.

Among the more established names in the league, DC United's original players tended to be Hispanic – with origins in Latin or Central American countries such as Bolivia and El Salvador – and the supporters were also primarily to be found among the Hispanic communities of Washington D.C. A typical supporter might be described as aged 30–35, male, and Hispanic.

The values associated with DC United on its formation in 1996 were that it was authentic and true to its beliefs. DC United was well run as an organization, and also focused on the game and its sporting aims.

In recent years, the competitive position in MLS has shifted so that the teams are now more on a par with each other. There are now many other good teams in the league, which is a challenge for DC United, but also has the positives of making the league more interesting.

MLS now contains a mix of well-established brands together with newly formed members such as Philadelphia and Seattle Sounders, which have made record-breaking starts to their major league careers, reaching the finals of the MLS Cup in November 2009.

As a brand leader, DC United has to continually look for ways to keep its brand fresh. DC United is nicknamed "the Black and Red" after the color of its shirts and shorts. The home kit has three white stripes on the shoulders to represent the three jurisdictions of the Washington Metropolitan Area – Washington DC, Virginia, and Maryland. These stripes were also originally on the front of the shirts.

The team "badge" or logo adopted in 1996 was a black bald

eagle facing to the right on three soccer balls, which were each on a star. Again these were to symbolize the three regions in the catchment area, and the bird is associated with the US federal government, which is based in Washington DC. Later the eagle was turned to face left and the stars changed to wing feathers similar to the stripes on the team's football strip.

Some versions also show gold stars to represent major sporting victories such as the MLS Cups (Doug Hicks, "D.C. United S.C.," FootballCrests.com <http://www.footballcrests. com/clubs/dc-united-sc>).

In May 2008, DC United announced a shirt sponsorship deal with Volkswagen. For many years DC United had not had a sponsor's name on its shirts because it had not found a sponsor that it considered to be consistent with its brand values. In announcing this partnership. United president and CEO Kevin Payne said, "We believe that the DC United brand stands for something significant and the 'brand' on the front of our jerseys has to be compatible with our vision. Volkswagen fulfilled and exceeded our wishes. They are a company committed to excellence and customer service with an international reputation for both" ("DC United and Volkswagen ink landmark sponsorship agreement," *Hispanic Wire,* May 8, 2008).

DC United also has outstanding issues to resolve in relation to its location and stadium. Since its formation, United has played at the RFK Stadium. Built in 1961, this stadium is the former home of the Washington Redskins (an American football team) and the Washington Nationals (baseball).

Plans to build the team's own stadium have been fraught with difficulties. A plan to develop a new stadium in Washington D.C. itself fell through, a later possibility in neighboring Maryland also did not take off, and in May 2009 fans of the club, which had an average attendance of 20,000 per match – third highest in the MLS – organized a protest march to try to raise political support for the club's stadium plans.

Media reports of the time commented:

MLS Commissioner Don Garber has officially weighed in on the topic, saying that if a stadium deal can't be reached, the team will be moved elsewhere – presumably to someplace that offers more political (read: financial) support. So what's the problem? Does the nation's capital really not want soccer? … somehow this fan base hasn't translated into political clout. They just can't seem to get a deal that will allow them to keep the team.

("DC United takes to the streets to try to keep the team in DC", May 8, 2009, http://www.theoffside.com/world-football/dc-united-takes-to-the-streets-to-try-to-keep-the-team-in-dc.html)

"D.C. United has long enjoyed a special relationship with our fans, who are the best in Major League Soccer," said United president Kevin Payne. "No matter what the need, we can always count on the unswerving support of our fans. It's no surprise that they've organized this march in support of our club. We hope the political leadership of the District, and the region, pay attention. We're sure the march and rally will be enthusiastic and friendly."

The importance of this to the fans of DC United can be seen by following this video link: http://www.dcunited.com/news-stats/new-stadium-effort

Some of the options include building a new stadium some distance from Washington DC, which might mean much greater traveling time to matches for fans.

The challenge of finding an appropriate location for a new stadium, and where this will be located in relation to Washington DC and the core fan base, is one of the major issues facing the future of DC United.

What's in a name?

Wimbledon Football Club was an English professional football club based in south-west London. From its beginnings as Wimbledon Old Central Football Club in 1889, the club spent decades as an amateur and semi-professional club before being promoted to the old English First Division in 1986. The club spent 14 years as a top-tier league club (from 1986 until 2000). During this time, Wimbledon became FA Cup winners in 1988, beating then First Division champions Liverpool 1–0.

After the publication of the *Taylor Report*, which called for the introduction of all-seater stadia in the aftermath of the Hillsborough disaster, Wimbledon took the decision to move away from its stadium, Plough Lane, as the cost of renovations to the stadium would be too great. An original temporary ground-share with south London club Crystal Palace lasted from 1991 to 2002. A number of different options were considered for a permanent home for Wimbledon FC. No suitable location was found near to the club's London roots.

Eventually, the club was given permission to move over 50 miles north to Milton Keynes, a new town built in Buckinghamshire. This decision was very unpopular with the club's fans and with English football fans generally, who believed that this move meant the club would no longer be the "real" Wimbledon. In response, a new "phoenix" club was formed, called AFC Wimbledon. This club has risen up the non-league pyramid so that it now plays in the Conference National (this league, known for sponsorship purposes as the Blue Square Premier, is the fifth league in English football, and only one tier below the top four professional English leagues).

After its move to Milton Keynes in September 2003, the original Wimbledon FC was renamed Milton Keynes (now MK) Dons. The renamed club now plays in Football League One (the third-tier English league), although it is not inconceivable that the two clubs may eventually end up as rivals at the same level.

In this case, the alienation of fans seems to have been based on the geographic shift that took place from London to Milton Keynes. This geographic shift is not in itself uncommon. In Rugby Union, London Wasps currently play at Wycombe. Football clubs have played in other geographic locations when there are problems with stadia. For example, Rotherham United are currently playing matches at the Don Valley Stadium in Sheffield, and Bristol Rovers contemplated sharing a ground with Cheltenham Town while its Memorial Stadium was redeveloped.

It seems that there are acceptable bounds for fans of a club.

Perhaps this is about how far away the club might be, whether this is temporary, and whether it is for a reason that the fans can understand and buy into.

In some cases, alienation of fans might come about not because of a geographic relocation, but because the club has behaved in some other way which is not deemed to be "in the true spirit" of the club. For example, some fans were not happy at the takeover of Manchester United by the Glazer family, and switched allegiance to a rival, FC United of Manchester. Leigh Railway Mechanics Institute (Leigh RMI) was in financial difficulties at the time, and asked to be taken over to form the new club. FC United has now reached the Northern Premier League, the seventh tier of English football (three below the Football League), and had an average attendance of 2,152 in the 2008–09 season. While this has declined from its height of 3,059 in 2005–06, the year of formation, FC United remained the 100th best-supported club in England in 2007–08. It should be noted that the club plays its home fixtures at Bury's Gigg Lane, so geography was not the trigger for disenchantment in this instance, but rather the hostile takeover of Manchester United. FC United is a supporter-owned club.

CHAPTER 2

Brand relationships in football

Brand equity in football

As explained in the Introduction, strong brands play an important role both financially and strategically for organizations. In discussing what constitutes a strong, or successful, brand, de Chernatony and McDonald (1998) comment that "A successful brand is an identifiable product, service, person or place, augmented in such a way that the buyer or user perceives relevant, unique, sustainable added values which match their needs most closely."

But what constitutes a "successful" brand in football? Brand Finance's 2009 report into the "Most Valuable European Football Brands 2009" (Soccerex Business, Q1 2009, p. 18), suggested that top-ranked Manchester United has a brand value of £329 million, up from £264 million in 2008 when it held second place. Second was Real Madrid with a brand value of £300 million (this is based on year end 2008 and might be increased by recent signings); Barcelona was third with a brand value of £266 million, and Bayern Munich, in fourth place with £247 million, considerably improved on its value of £147 million in 2008. Arsenal, Chelsea, AC Milan, Liverpool, Inter Milan, and Juventus were also ranked in the top ten.

The system used by Brand Finance in arriving at these brand valuations works in a way similar to credit rating of companies. Based on a set of measures specific to the sector – in the case of football these include brand awareness, revenue split, club heritage, European honors, UEFA ranking, and average attendances – the brand strength is assessed. The system works on the basis of calculating how much, if the company did not own the brand, it would have to pay to license it from a third party.

The dimensions used in this assessment of brand equity are

in many ways similar to those proposed by marketing literature. Aaker (1996) suggests that the measures should cover the full scope of the brand equity, including awareness, perceived quality, loyalty, and associations. Research into sport has identified measures for a number of these.

Awareness

In professional sports, this is largely down to the extent to which the club is covered by television and other media. Sport has the major advantage that there is uncertainty of outcome. An often-used example to explain this is that, while the film *Titanic* is enjoyable, even when it is seen for the first time, it is clear that the ship is going to sink at the end. In football the outcome is unknown, and that is what makes the game so compelling. Underdogs can and do win. Teams may under- and over-perform.

Among sports, football is an ideal format for today's audiences. Cricket or baseball matches over several days may not fit with hectic lifestyles (hence the introduction of shorter Twenty20 cricket matches). Some sports are complex and cannot readily be understood by those who do not know the game. Examples might include American football, cricket, and baseball. Football is 90 minutes long, the rules are simple, and most regions of the world have some version of the game. Even in regions that are not traditionally football-supporting such as the United States and India, there is a rise in interest. Although football, or soccer, tends to be viewed as a participation sport and a women's game in the United States (see Chapter 1, pp. 38–43 for more details), Major League Soccer (MLS) is still the fourth most supported league in the country, ranking equal to the NHL (National Hockey League) (Forbes 2008). In India, a youth market for football is emerging. Football coverage through satellite is expensive, so viewing tends to be in cafés and bars rather than at home, but there is also investment in youth academies (for example the co-operation between Manchester United's Soccer Schools and the All India Football Federation (AIFF) in a talent identification and development program (October 27, 2007: www.indiaexpress.com) so the market might increase.

The advent of the Internet has made football even more

accessible, and has opened up new possibilities for virtual communities of like-minded fans who can talk about their teams across continents and time zones.

Perceived quality

Deloitte and Touche (2009) shows a strong correlation between the quality of a club's squad (as measured by player wages) and the club's sporting performance. In academic literature, fans are found by economic studies to be more loyal to teams that are successful (see Baade and Tiehen 1990; Domazlicky and Kerr 1990). Loyalty is measured by both high average attendances and less variability in attendance. It should be noted that some football clubs have waiting lists for season tickets and so have virtually no variation in the number of fans attending home matches. Such waiting lists also tend to be common in successful teams, although a number of clubs have strong and loyal support despite, rather than because of, their on-the-pitch performance. Luton Town, for example, has just been relegated from the English Football League Two (fourth tier) into the Blue Square Premier League (fifth tier). This was not a result of poor performance but because of points deductions resulting from the financial difficulties and past conduct of directors of the club. Despite its relegation, Luton had still sold over 3,000 season tickets with 50 days to go before the start of the season. Average attendance in Football League Two was only 4,174 in the 2008–09 season.

Loyalty

Loyalty is beneficial to all businesses for a number of reasons. Reichheld (1997) argues that loyalty-based management must focus on retaining customers and employees to enhance profitability. The benefits of this approach, he argues, can be measured in terms of cash flow and hence profits. Profits from loyal customers increase over time. Sending thousands of letters, or even building databases to e-mail takes time and effort to generate a small proportion of responses. If a fan comes to a match as a result then there is a small return. If the fan returns to subsequent matches, buys a season ticket, or becomes an advocate and brings along others to matches, the value of that customer improves profits significantly. Marketing tends now to focus on the lifetime value of customers. It is then possible to work out how much the organization should invest in bringing in new customers, and in attempts to increase the loyalty of existing customers.

In football terms, Reichheld's argument would be that a loyal customer goes through stages of increasing value to a club:

- an initial return (such as ticket sale)
- increased volume of activity (more regular attendance, buying a replica shirt, spending at catering outlets)
- reduced marketing costs (season ticket only renewed annually so rate of communications may go down, customer may become involved in club-related activities unprompted)
- referrals (the customer brings in and may influence positively other customers)
- price premiums (highly committed individuals may become involved in sponsorship, corporate entertaining, even invest in the club).

Day (1969) proposed that brand loyalty had two components, a behavioral and attitudinal loyalty. This view, which was supported by later studies, was then used in relation to sports consumers by a number of studies, such as that of Backman and Crompton (1991) for people who played golf and tennis.

Customer-based brand equity in football

Studies of brand equity often have either a financial focus (how much is the brand worth?), or else a more strategic focus on improving the marketing efforts of an organization by making better decisions about target markets, brand positioning, and the marketing mix (service, price, place, promotion, people, physical evidence, and processes), which follow from these.

This latter approach is taken by Keller (1993), who calls this approach "customer-based brand equity." He contends that customer-based brand equity happens when a customer is "familiar with the brand and holds some favorable, strong and unique brand associations in memory."

The concept of customer-based brand equity has often been

used for studies of sports marketing, and seems relevant here to discussion of football brands, whose customers fit with the above definition.

Keller (1993) argues that customer-based brand equity depends upon a customer's brand knowledge. This, in turn, is made up of brand awareness (recall and recognition) and brand image (types of brand association, favorability of brand associations, strength of brand associations, and uniqueness of these brand associations). Keller later argues (2001) that customers ask of brands:

- Who are you? (brand identity).
- What are you? (brand meaning).
- What do I think or feel about you? (brand responses).
- What kind of association and how much of a connection would I like to have with you?

The following example of the repositioning of the League Managers Association brand discusses a members' association (representing football managers) which has gone through a recent process of considering what it is, what it stands for, and how it will build business-to-business relationships with other stakeholders in the football game.

The League Managers Association – The Managers' Voice

The first question which people consider when thinking about a brand for this type of football body is "why create a brand out of an organization such as the League Managers Association?" It is not a consumer product with an audience with whom an organization is trying to communicate. So why have a brand?

The history of the LMA

The League Managers Association (LMA) was created in 1992 as a support and service offering to its members. The six major aims of the LMA are:

- To represent the interests of the professional football

managers to the Football Association, Premier League, Football League and all the game's other governing bodies and stakeholders.

- To promote and publish the views of the professional managers on key issues within the game.
- To protect the rights and privileges of its members.
- To deliver and grow a range of support services to the managers both professionally and personally.
- To embrace and deliver strong commercial relationships with the game's sponsors and partners.
- To encourage honourable practice, conduct and courtesy in all professional activity.

The LMA will carry out all its activity with expertise, professionalism and integrity.

LMA – The Manager's Voice

The LMA has a solid platform based on strong affinity with its members. The tangible aspects of a brand – logo, brand guidelines, and so on – are very much the last part of a process which begins with the values and aims of the LMA.

The LMA exists to provide benefits for its members. These benefits include a set of core services, including legal, healthcare, relationship development, education, lifestyle management, career development, and help in any difficulties which might occur in the course of their careers.

For a members association, such as the LMA, the creation of a strong brand is important for three reasons:

- The brand is important in so far as it can help to improve the service offering to members. In order to achieve this, the LMA needs to maximize its economic or commercial development, with the aim of bringing in sufficient revenue to allow it to provide those services. The brand potential of the football managers as a collective group is based on the unique body of passionate people with extensive management and leadership experience. If this is done in a way that is not bounded by a sense of what fits with the values of the LMA, it could be potentially dangerous, so the creation of a clear and well-communicated set of values and guidelines for this activity is of benefit to the LMA.

- Historically, the LMA as an association has been less "visible" in the football community than many other of the game's stakeholders, such as the Professional Footballers' Association (PFA) and the Premier League, therefore the brand is the identity that can be used to symbolize the values of the LMA. A brand is a means of creating a "collective voice" for the LMA. In this way the brand can assist the organization in its desire to have a broader and more positive impact on the game. Essentially the LMA is a stakeholder in the game – and business – of football, and as such, has business-to-business relationships with other stakeholders within football. As well as being an organization, the LMA is essentially a lobbying group, for which it is useful to create a more visible and vocal identity. It is important that the LMA structures the way in which it grows its presence, and the process of thinking about how to do this plays an important role in successful achievement of its aims.

- The LMA spearheads the move to improve the brand of football management in this country (England). Football management is a turbulent, pressured role with a high profile which is an essential part of the football game. The LMA wishes to promote professionalism in football management – to enhance understanding and respect for the challenges of football management, and to promote it as a viable career option for which there are educational pathways, qualifications, and a basis in learning and professional development. Given these values it is important that the LMA itself moves forward in a considered and professional way.

Taking the brand forward

As a brand, the LMA has opted for a clear and simple approach. The LMA's identity is communicated by the logo opposite in the colors of black, green, and silver.

The strapline opposite represents the LMA's stated aim. Achievement of the aims of the LMA involves development

Figure 2.1 LMA logo

Figure 2.2 LMA strapline

and communication of its brand together with realizing the commercial potential of its brand in support of the organization's aims. To achieve this the LMA is engaging in a range of activities that will help it to take the brand forward.

The LMA does not rigidly follow a formal "brand custodian checklist," but it does apply a set of guiding principles that help it to decide which activities the organization should be involved in, or use its brand in conjunction with. These could be summarized as follows:

- Does this activity portray the LMA as an organization in a positive light?
- Does this activity portray the individual football managers in a positive light?
- Does this activity focus on football management and leadership in the context of the broader management field?
- Does this activity generate income?

Not every activity needs to tick all of these boxes, but these are useful guidelines for deciding whether an activity is likely to be consistent with the brand's aims.

The redesign of the LMA logo was also viewed in similar terms. The look of the brand and all marketing communications should look simple, high-quality, and be consistent.

A major question for an organization such as the LMA is "Who are its target markets?" The core audience of the LMA is clearly its membership, which buys or uses its services. All communications should be "member-centric," and building relationships with this membership is key.

The second aim of the organization, however, is that of being strong on behalf of this membership. In achievement of this aim, the game of football is the target audience. In putting forward the views and interests of the amazing body of people who are football managers, the LMA aims to be positive, proactive, and collaborative in its dealings with stakeholders within the game, be they football clubs, football bodies, or other stakeholders such as media.

The LMA aims to continue to increase awareness of the organization and what it stands for. To have a "voice" within the game of football, it is important that the LMA aims to achieve a positive PR profile. The CEO Richard Bevan has been very proactive, and is very good at taking up opportunities to put forward an LMA perspective on football issues. The intention is to ensure that the LMA is viewed as an integral part of the game of football.

Internal and external brand building

Commercial interest in the LMA brand tends to center on the football managers' role. There is massive interest in what football managers do. Some sponsorship interest in the LMA comes from companies such as Barclays and Castrol, which are already major sponsors of football (Barclays of the Premier League and Castrol of FIFA), and might add the LMA as part of their portfolio of football sponsorship because this supports their global sponsorship program and offers access to a "bundle of rights" such as attendance at LMA events – many of which provide unique opportunities and insights. One such dinner had a panel of Sir Alex Ferguson and Arsène Wenger discussing their views on a range of football issues; another, the President's Dinner, was hosted by LMA president and current England manager Fabio Capello; another was a tribute dinner for the late Sir Bobby Robson.

Alongside these events, the LMA has launched a management magazine, *The Manager*, and an annual conference, both of which move away from football to football management as part of the broader field of leadership and management. In putting football managers alongside business leaders in other fields, the credibility of the role of the football manager is reinforced. Given the intense interest in football management, both business and football management can gain from this type of collaboration.

The LMA has also invested considerable time and resource in its communication materials – such as DVDs, members' handbooks, newsletters, and e-newsletters – in order to increase continuing understanding of the organization, and to reinforce the brand and what it stands for. The materials all reflect the brand values, style, and are consistent with the aims and brand identity.

As brand identity and brand meaning have been debated in Chapter 1 of this book, this chapter concludes with a discussion of:

• What do I think or feel about you? (brand responses)

and

• What kind of association and how much of a connection would I like to have with you? (brand relationships)

Brand responses: What do I think or feel about you?

This section focuses primarily on football clubs as brands, and the different types of relationships that different types of fans have with these brands.

When talking about football fans, we tend to think about "diehard" fervent fans who live or die for their respective clubs. All kinds of different customers, however, can be important to clubs both as sources of revenue and for the support that they provide to the team. Alongside season ticket holders and other regular fans, occasional attendance at a match, a single corporate event, or a birthday treat provides resources to the club.

The priority for most clubs will be to identify those customers who are the mainstay of its market. These "bedrock" customers differ from other types of customers in terms of their loyalty to the club, and are more likely to be active in match attendance, buying merchandise, subscribing to club TV channels, and other types of activities.

Theories of consumer behavior have long recognized that customers are loyal to particular brands. Day (1969) first proposed that consumer loyalty should not just be understood in terms of buying and repeat buying. This behavior might be dictated by constraints such as availability, location, or price. Hence a customer might buy a particular brand of coffee because it represents value and is stocked by the nearest supermarket. This "spurious loyalty" in terms of a buyer's behavior or *behavioral loyalty* may not indicate any emotional attachment to a particular brand. Indeed a customer might be persuaded to buy a different brand if it were cheaper, if the supermarket changed its supplier, or the customer moved house to a new location.

Day defined "true loyalists" as those who had a "strong internal disposition" towards the brand. The two dimensions of *behavioral* and *attitudinal* loyalty formed the basis of later work in consumer behavior, by authors such as Dick and Basu (1994) and Kumar and Oliver (1997). This latter work also considered the process through which consumers develop loyalty:

- The first stage is *cognitive,* in which consumers collect and consider information about brands. Cognitive is defined by psychologists as being to do with the process of knowing (being aware and thinking) about a brand.
- The second stage is *affective,* in which consumers begin to attach feelings and emotions to a particular brand. Psychologists define affective as being influenced by or resulting from emotions.
- Finally, consumers reach a *conative* stage, in which they show the behavior of loyalty towards a brand. Psychologists define

conative (from the Latin verb *conari*, attempting or striving) as having a motivation, drive, or will to do something.

Once consumers reach the final stage of loyalty, the conative stage, they are likely to buy and continue to buy a particular brand and are less likely to search for alternatives, as they have already been through the process of evaluation and deciding (cognitive), and becoming emotionally attached (affective) to this particular brand. At this stage loyal consumers will most probably resist attempts to make them switch to a different brand, and may also act as advocates and generate positive "word of mouth" about the brand to others at an earlier stage of the process.

Defining attitudinal loyalty

Attitudinal loyalty involves emotional attachment to the brand rather than simply repeat purchasing. Dick and Basu (1994) define it as the extent to which feelings are engaged by a brand.

Defining behavioral loyalty

Behavioral loyalty has been defined as a "customer's consistent tendency to repurchase the same brand over time" (Jacoby and Chestnut 1978). Behavioral loyalty has been assessed using measures such as purchase rate behavioral loyalty (Aaker 1991). In football, someone who possesses a season ticket or attends more than a certain number of matches might be considered to have "behavioral loyalty" (Funk and James 2001).

Some authors argue that following a team through the media could also be considered as an indication of behavioral loyalty, as it may be difficult for some to attend matches, either because a venue has limited capacity or because geography makes frequent attendance difficult (Funk and James 2001; Gladden and Funk 2001).

Fan identification with football brands

In sports marketing and sports psychology studies, the concept of brand loyalty is often referred to as "identification," and "highly identified fans" are those who have strong loyalty to their chosen team.

Studies of how this loyalty, or identification, develops tend to be split into stages. The first of these is to identify the "motive" or trigger for the decision to support. Consumer behavior studies of sport tend to identify a list of factors that lead to support, then link these factors to the behavior of fans.

The first part of this section identifies a range of different triggers or motives for support. The section then goes on to explore how these translate into identification or loyalty to a particular club.

Motives for support

In their "Origins of Support" research in 2009, Eon, sponsors of the FA Cup, identified reasons why fans began to support a particular club. Among these influences are family connections with a particular club; if the person's father, mother, grandparent, or other family member was a supporter of a particular club, they might have played a positive influence in the decision on which team to support. From Eon's research, the influence of the father was most frequently mentioned, although mothers, grand-parents, and other family members also set some fans on the road to supporting a team. In football, the fan might develop a behavioral loyalty first. If a family member is already a big fan who regularly attends matches (that is, shows behavioral loyalty), the new fan might attend matches either without having any say in the decision, or without feeling any particular emotional attachment to the club, before beginning the process of actively deciding which – if any – club to support.

Given the extent of the loyalty of many football fans, it is relatively rare, but not unheard of, that children will decide that they are not interested in football, or else prefer to support a different team from their parents and siblings. In such cases, the new fan has simply gone through their own process of cognitive processing, and developed loyalty to a different team, or stopped before developing this loyalty.

Other reasons why fans decide to support a particular team include the influence of friends. If a child goes to school with fans of a different team or is surrounded by discussion of victories and star players of a different club, they may decide to fit in with the social group rather than their family.

Likewise, interest in a particular club can be triggered by a particularly memorable match. I am one of a generation of Sunderland fans who were influenced not only by local and family ties to the club, but also by Sunderland winning the FA Cup in 1973!

Additional motivations include a star player or coach being involved in a particular team. Loyalty to a particular player may be so strong that a fan without any other particular attachment to a particular club might switch allegiance to a new club when a player changes club. A fan who, for example, is particularly attracted by David Beckham as a player or personality might decide to follow Real Madrid when Beckham moved there from Manchester United, then move onto LA Galaxy and AC Milan as the player moves between clubs. In some cases, even if the main allegiance remains with Manchester United, this secondary motivation might explain phenomena such as support of "second clubs" (see Chapter 5, page 144).

It is interesting to note that similar motivations for support for particular football clubs can be found among fans who never achieve "behavioral" loyalty. Whether on the grounds of geographic distance, work, or their own sporting commitments, some fans might exhibit very high attitudinal loyalty but not attend matches. I once commented on the apparent irony of a Cyprus-based fan professing undying support for Manchester United. The fan (rightly) pointed out that this was grandfather–father–son third-generation support, and that the local supporters' club in Limassol was extremely active in support of the club, hosting events, including one involving the manager, Sir Alex Ferguson. However he did not have the opportunity for regular live match attendance.

With the globalization of football and the advances in digital media, fans with strong attitudinal loyalty and strong behavioral loyalty (in activities other than live match attendance) might reasonably be considered no less loyal than season ticket holders of a club (see Chapter 5 for further discussion of international fans).

Earlier contributions to understanding of the reasons why fans support sport include Sloan (1989), who points to emotions or psychological needs that are met by watching sport. These include stress and stimulation seeking, catharsis and aggression, entertainment, and achievement seeking. While the last of these was tested and supported by later research such as that of Cialdini et al. (1976), many of the others have either not been supported or have been contested by later studies which sometimes even suggest that, rather than being an outlet for aggression, watching sport can increase the levels of aggression.

Daniel Wann (1995) identified eight factors which he argued explained sport fan motivation. The Sport Fan Motivation Scale (SFMS) was made up of:

- **Eustress.** A positive form of stress which energizes people. Fans watch sports because they enjoy eustress or the excitement and anxiety which form part of the game (Branscombe and Wann 1994; Gantz and Wenner 1995; Prisuta 1979; Sloan 1989; Wenner and Gantz 1989).
- **Self-esteem.** Fans gain positive reinforcement of who they are and feel that their identity is enhanced by supporting their team (Branscombe and Wann 1992, 1994; Gantz 1981; Sloan 1989).
- **Escape from everyday life.** This temporary release from day-to-day worries and concerns has long been cited as a reason for sport support (Sloan 1989; Smith 1988).
- **Entertainment.** Watching sport may be a form of entertainment alongside alternatives such as theater, cinema, and watching television (Gantz 1981).
- **Economic factors based on financial gain through gambling.** The motivation to gamble on sporting events may prompt some individuals to follow the sport (Gantz and Wenner 1995; McPherson 1975).
- **Aesthetics.** Fans may find beauty and aesthetic value in watching some types of sporting performance (Sloan 1989; Smith 1988).
- **Group affiliation.** The social motivation to be with other people and to belong to the group may motivate some fans to support a team (Sloan 1989; Gantz and Wenner 1995). (This type of "belonging" is explored in more detail in Chapter 3, page 80.)
- **Family needs.** A related social motivation is that of spending time with other family members who share an interest in the sport (Gantz and Wenner 1995).

Source: Wann et al. (1999).

Research by Wenner and Gantz (1989) found that fans with pref-
erences for different sports showed different motivational styles.
So, for example, aesthetic motives might apply more to gymnastics, ice-skating, or athletics, whereas eustress might refer more
to sports with high tension. Wenner and Gantz argued that fans
were more likely to get "psyched up" by basketball than by baseball. Indeed team sports appealed more to individuals who had
eustress or escapist motivations. Economic motivations were also
linked more to aggressive sports (such as boxing and American
football) than to non-aggressive sports such as gymnastics. Interestingly, Wenner and Gantz classified football (soccer) as a non-
aggressive sport, possibly because it was positioned largely as a
women's sport in the United States at the time of their study.

The later Madrigal and Howard scale (FANDIM) scale (1995,
cited in Mahony et al. 2002) explored but reduced the eight factors
that Wann identified to four:

- suspense
- technical aspects
- vicarious achievement
- physical attraction.

Mahony et al. (2002) point to the fact that only two factors have
appeared consistently throughout research studies – eustress/
suspense and self-esteem/vicarious achievement.

Given the differences in motivations and the expected differences between motives for watching different sports, Mahony
et al. (2002) suggest that their study of motives for watching J
League football (Japan) should use a new scale. They excluded
Wann's (1995) "economic" motive together with physical attraction, which they did not feel to be very appropriate to football.
The seven factors included for football were:

- **Drama.** Spectators who are more interested in the game of
  football than in a particular team want to see interesting and
  closely contested matches. Most fans can imagine this type
  of motivation best if they think of themselves when they are
  watching a match as a neutral without particularly wanting one
  team to win. In this case, our interest is held by matches that

ebb and flow rather than a game in which one team wins by a large margin and the outcome is clear from the early stages of the game.

- **Vicarious achievement.** Fans often unthinkingly refer to themselves as playing a role in successful performances: "We outclassed them," "We were the twelfth man," while distancing themselves from poor performance "They were useless last night," "The manager got the team selection wrong," "The board ought to put their hands in their pockets." The response of football fans to good and poor performance is explored in greater detail later in this chapter (see page 71). There is considerable evidence that fans feel the successes of their team to be their own successes, and feel good about themselves when the team win. A chairman once described the "feel good" factor in the whole city after a good performance, compared with the atmosphere around the city in the bars and restaurants after a defeat. He even believed that productivity went up after a victory compared with after a defeat.

- **Aesthetics.** This refers to that overhead bicycle kick, the way in which the leading striker chipped the goalkeeper, or a heroic penalty save. Such moments are replayed and etch themselves on the consciousness of football fans. Many fans can recall in precise detail not only how these moments looked, but also the television or radio commentary that went with media coverage of these incidents.

- **Team attachment.** This is closest to the brand loyalty we might have to other types of organizations. The fan will develop an attachment to the club as an organization, to the squad of players, and to the coaching and management staff.

- **Player attachment.** Some fans are attracted to support a team because of a particular player who is playing for that team. This phenomenon can be seen clearly when a player of a particular nationality joins a club, and interest in that club from both fans and media from that country increases. When leading Japanese player Junichi Inamoto joined Arsenal, the number of Arsenal fans from Japan increased. Similar issues applied with South Korean fans of Ji-Sung Park and Manchester United, Greek fans of Bolton while Stelios played for the club, and Turkish fans of Blackburn who became interested as a result of Tugay playing for the club. Once that particular player has moved on from the club, the behavioral loyalty may switch to a different club or country. A legacy of loyalty may remain: the fan is no longer so actively interested, but still looks for the results for that club, or else the loyalty will end completely. In these cases, it is clear that there was no strong affiliation to the club as a brand, but rather to an individual player's brand.

- **Sport attachment.** As a neutral supporter, fan of another club, or fan of another sport, a fan may still enjoy watching a good, end-to-end football match. There is no particular affiliation to the club, but the experience of attending an interesting sporting event may still drive behavioral loyalty.
- **Community pride.** Many fans support a local team or a team associated with their family roots or a place where they have lived at some stage of their life. The role of geography in football brands is explored in greater detail in Chapter 3 (see page 72).

Motives for support and fan behavior

The second stage of consumer behavior in sports fan studies is to consider whether fans who support sport for different reasons then behave differently towards their chosen sport.

In their study of J League Football, Mahony et al. (2002) link the different motivations of J league fans to the length of time they have been fans and to the number of games attended.

There was a clear relationship between the length of time that someone had been a fan and their level of loyalty or "identification" with the team. Fans who had been involved with the sport for longer were more strongly attached to the team than fans who were early in their pattern of support. Interestingly, more recent fans were more motivated by support of a particular player than were fans of longer standing. Likewise, both aesthetics and the drama of the game (how close the game is) were more important to recent fans than to those who had been fans for longer.

More detailed insights into the nature of the identification with particular sports can also be gained both from the Sports Spectator Identification Scale (SSIS) (Wann and Branscombe 1993) and the Psychological Commitment to Team Scale (PCT) (Mahony,

Madrigal, and Howard, 2000). The SSIS (Wann and Branscombe 1993) contains seven Likert-scale items which assess identification with sports teams. Response to these items ranges from 1 (low identification) through to 8 (high identification). So for example, an item might be a question such as "How important to you is it that the team you support wins?" Originally based on data from basketball, the SSIS scale was validated in 2001 by Wann et al.

Mahony et al.'s PCT scale contains 14 items to assess a sports fan's loyalty to, or identification with, their preferred sport. The concept of brand loyalty, or identification, in football and the classifications of sports and football fans are discussed in the remainder of this chapter.

Brand relationships – What kind of association would I like to have with you?

Research suggests that consumer loyalty to sports teams is much stronger than that shown towards other types of brands such as beer or chocolate (Sebastian and Bristow 2000).

That said, among those who attend football matches, not all will be loyal fans and followers of the club. Revenue will also be generated by clubs from occasional attendees of matches, those who have come along for social reasons, even fans of other clubs. These individuals are referred to here as spectators rather than fans. Fans and fandom have attracted particular attention, given that "who is the most loyal fan of all" is a preoccupation of rival fans, and even within the fan base of football clubs.

The assumption in this book is that there is a distinction between:

- A *spectator*, who is someone who watches and may enjoy a particular sporting event without any change to their cognitive (thought), affective (feeling), or conative (wish to do something) behavior: that is, without having or developing a particular loyalty to the brand. They enjoy the sporting spectacle itself.
- A *fan*, who is someone with a strong loyalty to the particular club or individuals within the club (Koo and Hardin 2008). The attachment is often emotional, as well as possibly social.

Dimensions of sports fan loyalty

Based on Day's (1969) classification, adopted by Backman and Crompton (1991) and other studies of sports fans, Mahony et al. (2000) classified sports fans according to their attitudinal loyalty (or psychological attachment) to the team, as well as by their behavioral loyalty (or active participation in the sport or in watching the sport).

In football terms, *behavioral loyalty* might include attending matches, wearing team colors, watching televised football matches, buying club merchandise, and other actions involving the team and its support. Fans who show this type of behavioral loyalty might also have attitudinal loyalty, although this is not always the case. For example, a parent might buy a football shirt for a child even though they do not have any psychological commitment to the team themselves, and a fan might attend a match to fit in with peers or for other social reasons without having any psychological attachment.

Attitudinal loyalty is the extent to which the feelings of the individual are engaged with the particular brand. Those with some degree of attitudinal loyalty are of more interest to marketers in all fields. In football, attitudinal loyalty can be extreme, with fans continuing to attend matches of teams through extremely unsuccessful periods in their history. This can be very positive for marketers of football brands, who are managing brands whose customers feel very attached to them. The attachment can be much more intrinsically linked with the customer's sense of "self" than most types of brands. This may boost interest, identification, and willingness to purchase products and services connected to the brand. People with strong attitudinal loyalty to something also tend to pay more attention and notice the adverts and messages about the object of their attachment.

Conversely, extreme attitudinal loyalty in football can have negative consequences. This strong emotional attachment might have a dark side that leads some fans to negative behavior such as violence towards rival fans. (The dark side of highly identified fans is discussed later in this chapter on page 75.)

Why do we need to understand identification and loyalty?

Understanding the differences behind the motives of fans and spectators in attending a live sports event helps to provide understanding of the different strategies for their needs, and helps both clubs and fans. Clubs gain understanding of how they might motivate fans to attend more matches and meet the needs of different types of fans. Fans can gain a better relationship with the clubs they support, and gain access to the information and services that are of interest to them, which should improve their enjoyment of the game.

Sports marketing presents a number of frameworks that offer insights into fans, and how loyal or identified they may be with a particular team. The first of these is that of Mahony et al. (2000), which uses Day's behavioral and attitudinal loyalty framework (1969) to classify sports fans.

- Fans who have strong psychological (attitudinal) loyalty and strong behavioral loyalty are considered to be *"true loyalists."*
- Fans who have low psychological and behavioral loyalties are *not loyal*.
- Between these two extremes, fans who show strong behavioral loyalty (frequent attendees) but who are low in attitudinal loyalty or psychological commitment are described as *"spurious loyalists."*
- Fans with strong attitudinal or psychological commitment but low behavioral commitment are *"latent loyalists."*

The above framework is not specific to football, but helps to offer insights into the different levels and types of loyalty that a fan might show to a sport.

Research has also looked at football fans and how they might be segmented or classified. The work of Tapp (2004) and Tapp and Clowes (2002) looks at how behavioral and attitudinal loyalty differ, and considers what this means for football. Giulianotti (2002) draws theories from sociology rather than marketing, discussing fandom, different types of fans, and what they feel that they gain from being a fan. Other classifications look at whether it matters to fans how well their team performs and the impact that this has on the support decisions (Bridgewater and Stray 2002).

These classifications help to provide a clearer picture of the ways in which football fans can be segmented. It is easy to work out who they are, where they live, what they do for a living, or the type of lifestyle they have. These types of data are often contained in club databases and season ticket lists. As in other sectors, however, it is not always easy to understand why someone supports a club and what motivates their support behavior. Why does a fan attend a certain number of matches? Why are some matches more attractive than others? Why would someone stop supporting or stop attending?

Without answering "why" questions a club cannot create the classic benefit segmentation proposed by Haley (1968) as being the optimal way of understanding a set of customers.

Classifications which look at "why" (Tapp and Clowes 2002; Tapp 2004) build on marketing research by Day (1969) and Mahony et al. (2000) to help clubs understand different types of loyalty behavior among football fans. Loyalty status is important to fans. As Tapp puts it, "How many shoppers will sing 'loyal customer' as they make their weekly trip to Asda?" but football fans are often preoccupied with showing that they are more loyal than someone else because it adds to their sense of self-worth and belonging to the group. As a result fans tend to overstate how loyal they are, and it can be difficult to get a true picture.

Tapp notes that many fans who consider themselves as loyal do not attend matches regularly. In attendance terms they would seem to be occasional or "casual" fans. His segmentation, based on the work of Dick and Basu (1994), divides fans based on their attitudinal and behavioral loyalty into four categories (see Figure 2.3).

Carefree casuals (Mahony et al.'s *not loyal*) are low on behavioral or attitudinal loyalty and so are of little interest to marketers. It may, however, be interesting to understand why they do not become more committed fans. For these fans football is entertainment. Tapp reports one such fan as saying, "I can take it or leave it to be honest. It's entertainment on a Saturday. We wake up in the morning and think – shall we go to the footy today?"

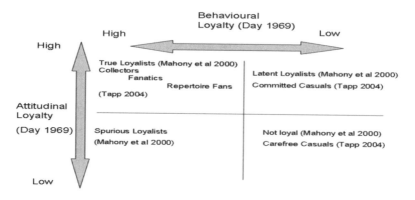

Figure 2.3 Classifying football fan loyalty

For these fans the attraction of football might be outweighed by other choices.

Committed casuals (Mahony et al.'s *latent loyalists*), in contrast, are fans with high attitudinal loyalty – they consider themselves to be loyal fans of the club even though they do not frequently attend matches. One particular group of these fans had recently decided not to renew their season tickets. Some said this was because they led complicated lives or were unable to justify the expenditure at that time. They were not in any way dissatisfied with the team. Reasons for casual support are working and family commitments, geography, and financial constraints.

Good conditions for loyal support included a long tradition of previous support, and older and more settled fans with fewer commitments to work or young families. Income seemed to have some, but not too strong a relationship with loyal support. Many fans made considerable sacrifices to afford their season tickets and follow the team to away matches. This pattern is comparable to that identified for Premier League fans in 2000, wherein the fan base of Sunderland AFC has different groups of fans with similar levels of income, differing in age and the reasons they support the club.

Switching behavior

Tapp and Clowes (2002) did not find any fans who admitted to switching teams or supporting more than one team, perhaps

Segmentation: the fan base of Sunderland AFC

Even within a single club and among the fans who regularly attend matches, distinct groups of fans exist. In the 2000–01 season, the following groups of fans could be seen within the fanbase of Sunderland AFC. A fifth group of fans was identified who did not attend matches because of work or distance from the ground.

The highest loyalty in behavioral terms was described by the time by Sunderland AFC as its "bedrock" support. Here this could be split into two parts:

- The first group, "die-hards," were the salt of the earth. These fans attended regularly, are loyal, passionate, and very emotionally attached to the club. They contain a high percentage of season ticket holders of the club.
- The second group were also loyal supporters but their attachment to the club seemed to be more negative. For want of a better description these fans could be nicknamed the "Hecklers!" They are equally as emotionally attached as die-hards, and had a similar demographic profile, but their relationship seemed negatively rather than positively charged. These fans were pessimistic about performance and very concerned about finances. The spirit of this group is captured by Nick Hornby in his comment:

I have begun to relish the misery that football provides ... I have been cold and bored and unhappy for so long that when the team is good I feel slightly, but unmistakably, disoriented.

(Hornby 1992: 245)

In addition to these fans, regular attendees also contained:

- The third group who could be labeled the "professionals" were older and higher income than the two most attached groups. These fans had average levels of emotional and social ties to the club, and there was an average number of season ticket holders (41 percent) among their number. These are the type of fans of whom Williams harshly says, "An ersatz following of promiscuous customers, with no real footballing tradition" (Williams 1996: 3), but they seem to have a real attachment to the club in this instance, although their level of identification is somewhat lower than the first two groups.

- A fourth group is "youth." This group is distinctly younger than the other groups. These fans also contain a high number of season tickets. Perhaps they come with families? They have a more social than emotional connection to the club.
- The fifth group did not often (or maybe ever) attend matches. They are known here as "E Loyal" and they are perhaps the most interesting. Some cite work reasons for their non-attendance, others have become expatriates. Most have a historical connection with Sunderland. They are interesting in that they are older, higher income, and very active. It is likely that they would be very interested in merchandise, websites, and other information about the club, as they cannot get enough information. They are more knowledgeable than any other segment, perhaps in compensation for their lack of attendance, to prove their "true fan" status. These are the "attitudinally" loyal fans, and they also show behavioral loyalty in support behavior other than that of physically attending matches.

because fans do not wish to admit to this type of support. While the notion of switching teams is abhorrent to most fans, it does, however, appear in the work of Mahony et al. and that of Stewart and Smith (1997). Tapp and Clowes (2002) also discuss the possibility that there are "repertoire" fans sitting alongside the more common "one club" fans. Kahle, Kambara, and Rose (1996) find this type of behavior, suggesting that among those who enjoy a sporting spectacle, or football in general, there may be fans who, for whatever reason, do not develop a particularly strong affiliation to a particular team and enjoy different allegiances throughout their football supporting life.

An English colleague once explained how he felt that he had missed out in his formative years, having not been brought up in this country and not have developed a passion for a particular football team. His children who do have this type of allegiance and other fans find it difficult to understand how someone could be interested in football generally without having developed their kind of burning football passion.

Tapp also introduces the idea (2002) that loyalty can feed inwards on itself and be independent of the team. "We are loyal supporters" takes on a momentum that goes beyond the specifics of the club, and is to do with the self-image of the fans themselves. The idea of "die-hard" versus "fair-weather" fans implies that "true" fans are loyal irrespective of how well that team is doing. Variation in attendances depending on how well the club is doing suggests that some fans do stop attending when teams do badly even if they remain "loyal" in terms of their latent interest in the club. For many, however, demonstrating loyalty becomes an end in itself. This idea is supported by Bristow and Sebastian (2001), who identify a group of fans who see themselves as loyal despite the performance of the team.

The typology developed by Stewart and Smith (1997) for Australian Rules football – later applied to football by Quick and Leuwen (1998) – builds the concept of performance into the basis for five groups of fans:

- Aficionado   Seeks quality performance. Loyal to the game not a team.
- Theatre goer   Seeks entertainment and wants a close contest.
- Passionate partisan Wants the team to win, identifies with successes and failures.
- Reclusive partisan Identifies strongly with a team but does not often attend.
- Champ follower   Changes allegiance to teams who win.

Fans switching their support to more successful teams are negatively referred to as "glory hunters," and tend to be despised by other fans. So perhaps it is not surprising that Tapp and Clowes (2002) did not find fans owning up to this type of switching. They did, however, find a number of fans who admitted they watched other teams as well as their main team. This might be a local non-league team, attending other matches when the preferred team was playing away from home. The concept of second team support is also found among international football fans (see Chapter 5), who might support a second team if their own team is not playing in a particular tournament, or who might support both a local team – whose matches they attend – and an international team that they follow via television or the Internet.

Marketing strategies and different types of fans

Mahony et al. (2000) suggest strategies that clubs might use to market effectively to fans with different types and levels of loyalty.

Appealing to spuriously loyal fans

Spuriously loyal fans (who attend matches but do not feel a strong attachment) appear on club databases to be just as loyal as true loyalists who are high on both dimensions. They attend matches, watch matches as frequently but perhaps for different reasons (maybe family or friends are true fans, or they are true fans of another team in a different location, which is too far away for them to attend matches regularly). A number of students are spurious football supporters, and also football fans of clubs too far away to attend might be persuaded to come to their local club because of reduced price tickets, as a social outing, and because they miss involvement in being a "fan."

Spuriously loyal fans will stop supporting if there is something better on offer, or maybe if performances drop off and the football is not attractive. Based on the research of Sheth (1987), Mahony et al. (2000) suggest trying to increase the psychological commitment of this type of fan. Perhaps clubs could provide fans with good reason to feel more psychologically committed to the club, such as excellence of service, the fan-friendliness of the team, or maybe a great new signing, with whom the fan can identify.

Alignment marketing is also suggested. Here the organization builds a link in the fan's mind with social causes or other values that are important to the fan beyond football. For example, the club could build a link with a particular charity, develop its contribution in the community, work to strengthen the diversity of its fan base, and demonstrate a greater value that appeals to the fan on a higher level.

Appealing to latent loyal fans

These fans are very attitudinally or psychologically committed but do not show strong behavioral loyalty. It may well be that there are good reasons these fans do not attend matches regularly. Chapter 5 describes this type in international markets who are geographically unable to attend. They may demonstrate behavioral loyalty through wearing club shirts or watching matches on television. In some cases, fans fall into this group because the costs of attending matches are too great. For this type of fan the suggested strategy is to "eliminate barriers" (Sheth 1987). This might mean using technology to make match coverage available, or price incentives to fans who cannot afford to attend matches. So reduced prices for some matches, family discounts, availability of finance for season tickets, half season ticket options, or grouping "mini tickets" of a particular set of matches at the same rate around the availability of fans might be options.

Building relationships with loyal fans

These are the core of a club, and without their loyal and undying support the club could not continue to exist. Most clubs have a name for their "true" loyalists: the "die hards," "bedrock support," and so on.

Classifying Premier League fans by type of loyalty

The example earlier in this chapter categorizes fans of Sunderland AFC into distinct groups depending on the level of their loyalty or identification with the club.

Data can also be compared across the Premier League (this is based on the clubs that were in the league in 2000–01) to see whether, for example, some have fans who are more emotionally or socially attached, or whether some fans are more concerned with tradition than others. Note that not all clubs were included in this analysis, only those where the number of fans who participated in the study was sufficiently great for statistical analysis.

When the clubs are grouped according to the average score for each brand value, they fall into three distinct groups which are interpreted below:

- **Group 1: Sunderland, Aston Villa, Newcastle, Ipswich.** Team success has a lot of emotional significance for the fans. They were quite concerned whether the team won or lost (a mid-level of impact on their self-esteem), and their behavior was heavily affected by the level of performance. Good results led to increased involvement with the brand. History and tradition were considered quite important by fans.
- **Group 2: Middlesbrough, Southampton, Manchester City.** Team success had a mid-level of emotional significance. Fans were very active in attending matches, they felt less personally affected (self-esteem) by the level of performance than the previous group, and were less concerned also about history and tradition.
- **Group 3: Manchester United, Tottenham, Liverpool, Chelsea, Everton.** Match attendance was extremely important to these fans as a social activity. Success was also important. Fans were knowledgeable about their clubs, but overall the emotional tie ranked lower than the social side of support.

It is not clear why and how fans fall into these groups, but cluster analysis shows that these groups are distinctly separable (Bridgewater and Stray 2002).

Loyalty in sports fans is often referred to as the level of "identification" between the fan and the sports brand.

Highly identified fans are the most interesting type of football fans to football marketers as they are the most likely to buy season tickets, merchandise, highlights packages, and even to contribute financially to clubs in times of hardship. Loyalty and level of identification is also a topic which fascinates fans themselves, as they spend an amount of their football-supporting lives in trying to demonstrate to fans of their own and other clubs their "loyalty status."

Highly identified sports fans consider themselves to be the true or "real" fans of a club. Their identification with the brand results in affective, cognitive, and behavioral association with the brand. They are most likely to attend matches, buy merchandise, help out at club events, or even become involved in ownership of the club through buying shares or through supporters groups.

Marketing literature suggests that clubs should make sure that their most loyal fans are not neglected in the pursuit of new, or younger, fans, but that the relationship between loyal fans and the club continues to develop. Loyalty is rewarded in some ways, as fans who buy more tickets – season ticket or part-season ticket holders – get lower prices per match than those who just attend occasionally. This relationship can be developed still further if the club makes the fan feel valued and part of the club. This might be helped by personalized communication, VIP loyalty schemes, or privileged access to events with players and club staff based on the level of loyalty that the fan shows to the club.

Chapter 4 explores the idea of a brand or service experience where club and fan interact with each other and continue to develop and reinforce the relationship.

The dark side of highly identified fans

High levels of identification between sports fans and a particular club are usually seen as positive. These are seen to result in increased participation, attendance at events, purchase of merchandise, and other positive engagements with the team.

High identification can, however, result in less positive behavior, which Wakefield and Wann (2006) refer to as the "dark side" of highly identified fans.

The negative behaviors associated with high levels of identification are excessive complaining and confronting others, possibly either fans who are not seen to be as loyal or rival fans. This behavior may also be linked with drinking at events, shouting at officials, the manager, board, or players, and violence. Gibson et al. (2002) comment that these fans "have arguably taken identification to the extremes" to become dysfunctional.

While sports team identification is generally found to be good for communities (see Chapter 3, page 90), because it helps and encourages community integration (Melnick 1993) and helps to build individual and collective self-esteem (Wann 1994), in a minority of cases high levels of identification seem to spill over into negative behaviors.

Research suggests that these fans are no more or less highly identified with their teams than other fans whose behavior is good and positive.

The "dark side" of high identification can span a whole range of behaviors including:

- Excessive complaining. These are the fans who express their negative views loudly to players, coaching staff, and match officials.
- Obsessing about the performance of their team, ringing into radio phone-ins and complaining on websites about some aspect of performance even if the team won (but not by enough goals, or without keeping a clean sheet, or why did the manager have to begin with that starting line-up?). Research by Wakefield and Wann (2006) suggests that a majority of the fans who dominate the airwaves on football and sports phone-ins are dysfunctional!

While this type of behavior is irritating or a source of "get a life" type of amazement, it has no lasting negative consequences. At the other end of the scale, the following can also be characteristics of highly identified "dysfunctional" fans:

- aggression and confrontation
- violence to players, staff, rival, or even fellow fans
- hooliganism.

Some research suggests that crowd violence or hooliganism occur among fans showing that they are part of the "in-crowd" (Dunning, Murphy, and Williams 1986). Wakefield and Wann (2006) however suggest that this is happening because of individual dysfunctional behavior, and would find an outlet in any case. In their study of American football fans, the authors found that the wish to complain and confront went well beyond the game and its outcome, and might involve complaining about non-sport areas of the club, and even intentional trips to confront rival fans. In these cases, it appears that the dark side of highly identified fans does not stem from their levels of identification with the football club, but from "deeper, more troubling, personal characteristics (for example, chronic anti-social attitudes and behaviors) that emerge not only in the sports setting, but likely elsewhere" (Wakefield and Wann 2006: 179).

What do fans do when they are unhappy with football brands?

This emotional attachment to a football brand may result in different behavior than for other types of brand. If a customer has a bad experience with a brand of car, or a coffee brand, then the customer is likely to respond by switching to a different brand. Marketers aim to "lock" customers into loyalty and remaining with their brand, although there is recognition that high customer expectations and competition may result in brand switching.

With sports brands, Cialdini et al. (1976) suggested that switching behavior was unlikely. Although the previous section highlights some types of fans and some situations in which fans may switch their allegiance, a majority of fans would not switch the team that they support no matter how poor the performance. Even in Sunderland's then-record low 15-point season of 2005–06 in the Premier League, fans would not contemplate switching allegiance to Newcastle United. The nature of attitudinal loyalty in football makes this out of the question.

A deeply emotional response to good and poor performance in sports brands does, however, exhibit itself. Cialdini describes the emotional response to good performance as BIRGing (basking in reflected glory) and to bad as CORFing (cutting off rejected failure).

When fans BIRG they wish to associate themselves with the brand, claim credit, and *internalize* success: "We were the twelfth man!"

There is a sense of vicarious achievement, improved mood and self-esteem. When fans CORF, the manager, players, board, and referee were all responsible for this failure – "We were robbed, the manager should be sacked" – but the fans are not responsible, even if they heckled a player so much that his performance became worse. This is *externalizing* failure, and may not be done consciously but is done to protect the fan's self-esteem.

Fans report that they might actively avoid TV highlights, match write-ups, and web boards that they frequent after a good performance. The emotional tie to the brand makes the pain of association too great. This wish to put a distance between themselves and the source of their pain may explain variations in match attendance. Refusing to attend a match, even ripping up season tickets, might be an emotional outlet for the fan in the case of perceived poor performance of the team.

CHAPTER 3

Understanding the football "brandscape"

The environment surrounding a football brand is made up of a number of different stakeholders who influence the success of the brand. Chapter 2 focused on the challenges arising from brand relationships with customers.

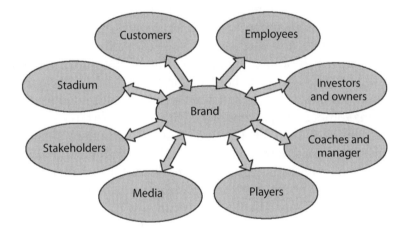

Figure 3.1 The football "brandscape"

This chapter reviews the challenges arising from each of the dimensions of the football brandscape.

Stadium

The physical facility itself plays a role in determining how good the group experience is.

There may be history and tradition attached to the stadium, so that the rituals of attending matches, where a fan sits, what time they go onto the concourse at half time, which bar or social area they meet in, may become part of the football experience. Fans may feel themselves bonded into a group beyond their immediate friends as part of a larger crowd. Comments such as "The crowd was the twelfth man that night" are not uncommon.

For many individuals, football is not just an entertainment and leisure activity but provides a sense of community and family. This phenomenon is common to many sports. In US sports marketing literature (Underwood, Bond, and Baer 2001), then owner of the Pittsburgh Steelers American football team, Dan Rooney, said that Steelers fans "have a wonderful sense of belonging to a family." One of the fans reported that his fellow fans were "almost blood relations" (Thurow 1997).

Some features of this sense of belonging are attributed to the physical facilities themselves. Studies have focused on service features such as cleanliness, safety, aesthetics, crowding, parking, seating comfort, and catering facilities (Wakefield and Blodgett 1994). All of these are dimensions that a club must get right. They do not only affect the decision to go back to the ground again or on how good the fan perceives the service quality to be, they may impact on perceptions of the brand itself.

Names such as Old Trafford, Emirates Stadium, Stamford Bridge, Anfield, Bernabeu, the San Siro, and the *Camp Nou* conjure up images among their fans not just of the buildings themselves, but also of moments of high tension, sadness, and elation. Stadia are worshipped by fans. Fans can now be married and have their ashes scattered at many football stadia. The significance of football stadia is reflected in the names given to them by their fans – and those of rival fans. Boca Juniors Stadium in Argentina is affectionately referred to as *La Bombonera* (the chocolate box), River Plate's stadium as *El Monumental*, Manchester United's Old Trafford as the Theatre of Dreams. Recent reaction to the possibility of changing the name of Newcastle United's St James' Park to that of a sponsor's name shows the strength of emotional attachment that fans may have for a football stadium and what it signifies.

When stadia close and clubs relocate, it is not uncommon for fans to buy sections of turf, turnstiles, the seat in which they sat, the barrier they leaned on. Many comment that there aren't many buildings in life that you become really attached to, perhaps a family home, but in some cases these stadia have been home to generations of fans. When Leicester City moved from Filbert Street in 2002, a senior academic colleague insisted on a late-night detour via the ground to show us the stand that he had stood in, and donated me a brick as a souvenir of the stadium that held so many memories for him!

Stadia are an opportunity for clubs to reinforce brand associations with fans. Although new and functional, a surprising number are still blank canvases which could be used more creatively to feature past players, victories, multimedia, colors, and logos to capture the atmosphere and tradition. Chapter 4 explores the concept of brand experiences in greater detail.

While stadia have improved greatly in recent decades, for example in England as a direct result of improvement suggested by the Taylor Report, there are still occasional stadia that do not measure up to standards, and the stadium itself can contribute to negative feelings and even violence between supporters. The physical attributes of stadia play an important role both in brand experiences and the quality of football as a service (see page 98).

Stakeholders

There are a number of stakeholders in football who influence a fan's experience of the brand. This may include rival fans, investors and owners of clubs, the media, and employees of the club such as stewards and catering staff.

Players

The actions of players both on and off the pitch can help to reinforce, or conversely can damage, the brand image and values of a club. A risk of any brand linked to a personality is that the individual's behavior becomes linked to the brand. So when players make themselves available to speak at fans' forums, attend the local children's hospital at Christmas, or go to local schools to support community football events, they are sending out a strong signal about the values that are important to the club. If they fall out of a nightclub, and worse, are pictured by media doing so, their actions damage not just themselves, but also the club's brand. The impact on a brand of the behavior of individuals with which it is associated may last longer than any individual player is at a club. For this reason, football owners and management must make it very clear to players that they have a duty as role models to young fans and to the club to behave in ways that are consistent with the brand.

The celebrity status and skills of players can significantly enhance the value of a club's brand. Marketing literature recognizes that customers – particularly those in Generation X and Y (today's youngsters and those now in their 20s) have grown up bombarded with so many marketing messages that they can filter these out very effectively. A brand may benefit from the emotional values that it places on a particular star. If they are heroic, athletic, good looking, or passionate, these values become linked in a customer's mind with the brand by association.

Sports stars become heroes, not just locally but sometimes nationally or even globally. As far back as 1889, Thomas Carlyle argued that heroes are a "human approximation of gods." Increasingly though, heroes are not seen in religious terms but modern-day human terms. Gods are above having to take human responsibility for their actions, and with hero status, modern football players have to accept the responsibilities that come with being a role model (Hughson 2009a). Humans may have weaknesses but "feet of clay" do not mean that fans see them as lesser heroes (Hughes-Hallett 2004). In their introduction to the excellent *Dangerous Book of Heroes*, authors Iggulden and Iggulden (2009) say of the heroes whose stories they tell, "Some of the heroes in this book are more rogue than angel – and one or two are absolute devils. Yet in their brief existence they showed what can be done with a life."

It is in this light that sporting heroes must be seen. Fans respond to their on the pitch exploits even though, in some cases, the individual may have weaknesses or character flaws. Perhaps these serve to make them less perfect and easier for real people to identify with.

Literature often features stories of heroes. Literary theorists have identified types of heroes that particularly appeal to readers.

Among these, Hughson (2009a) picks out *prowess heroes* and *moral heroes* as being closest to sporting heroes.

The *prowess hero* is defined by Coffin and Cohen (1978) as being a "doing hero" whose feats were talked about by people of a particular time by whatever means of communication was common at the time of their actions. In current times this would be discussion of football in newspaper, radio, and TV reports as well as on Internet message boards. Sporting prowess can be captured by visual media so that ever better slow-motion replays can enhance live action and be replayed via You Tube and other media to vast numbers of fans who may not have seen the exploit in person.

Moral heroes are those who show particular bravery, heroism, or moral character, and stand above the levels achieved by the majority of people. If the sporting hero does not just "do" well but shows a particular style or character is doing so, he may be elevated to this type of heroic status in the eyes of fans. Sunderland fans still recount the story of one such hero, their chairman Niall Quinn, who spoke on behalf of fans who were refused access onto a flight home from an away match – for allegedly singing raucous songs in support of the chairman when he and the board got onto the same flight – and sorted out arrangements for all fans to get home (from Sunderland to Cardiff, a distance of 320 miles) by taxi. A particular speech ("These are my people") is still used as a signature by individuals on the fans' message board www.readytogo.net, and the story provides part of the heroic status of the previous star player who has gone on to lead the club.

Hughson (2009a) further goes on to identify particular types of sporting hero, including:

- **The anti-hero.** This category is seen as far back as Ancient Greek times. Good looks and charm may be associated with this type of hero, whose behavior may not always endear them to fans. So John McEnroe, tennis champion, might be more remembered for his off-the-pitch tantrums, Andy Murray may attract comments for his terse style in interviews. In football, players whose off-the-pitch lifestyle lets down their on-the-pitch talent might be viewed as examples of the anti-hero.

- **The showman.** Some sports stars are famous for the style with which they perform. Many of those who saw Pelé, George Best, Brian Clough, or Bobby Charlton play will extol the way in which they played in a particular match, or the ease with which they beat opposition players or scored goals.
- **The scientist.** Yet other types of players attract attention because of their technical expertise. David Beckham's ability from a dead ball, Rory Delap's long throws, or the Holland team's "total football" might be less flamboyant than the showman, but they are equally important to success.

We are increasingly interested in heroes. Modern society turns even reality TV stars and ordinary people into celebrities, and so is fascinated by sporting heroes. Celebrity endorsement works because the cultural meaning (which the customer sees the celebrity as embodying) is transferred to the product or service that they are endorsing (McCracken 1989). Buying a star football player benefits a football club not just – it is hoped – by improving the quality of the playing team, but also by enhancing the football brand. For this reason many players' contracts now contain agreements on sums of money that the player will be paid for use of his image by the club. These "image rights" are discussed in more detail below.

The impact of introducing a celebrity player into an organization is not always positive. As with any celebrity endorsement, the organization runs the risk that the individual will behave in a way that brings negative publicity to the club's brand, or that fans will decide that they do not like the "cultural meaning" of the player. In this case customer perceptions of the whole brand and organization become negative (Langmeyer and Shank 1993), and the impact can be long term.

Research into the impact of sports stars as endorsers of both sports and other types of products (Koerning and Boyd 2009) reaches some interesting conclusions:

- First, famous athletes were more effective at endorsing a sports brand than those who were not famous. They did not, however, improve the image of the product they were endorsing, but their own image.

- Second, the endorsement worked best when there was a "fit" or match between the endorser and what was being endorsed.

In football terms, it is unsurprising that star players have most impact because fans perceive them in the most positive light. In general, football stars only have impact on customers if the customers know who they are. The iconic status of a star, such as David Beckham, means that he is as effective in endorsing Calvin Klein underwear, Gillette Razors, or LA Galaxy. But do fans notice the product or brand that is endorsed, or do they simply register David Beckham? Research suggests that while celebrity endorsement has an impact, there is a danger that the celebrity overshadows the brand being endorsed.

Koerning and Boyd's study (2009) says that "matching" is important. In other words, athletes are better endorsers of sports products than other types of product. So football players would be expected to be most effective at promoting the brand of the football club rather than other types of product. The key question, however, will be whether they are raising their own status rather than that of the club. Again, the star player might overshadow the club brand.

This raises interesting questions about the long-term impact of the *galácticos* strategy, as revived by President Perez, for the Real Madrid brand. In revenue terms, celebrity *galácticos* players will boost merchandise sales, as the global fan base will want to buy a Kaká or Ronaldo, Real Madrid shirt. Impact on ticket sales is likely to be low, given that the Bernabeu is so full that not even all of the *socios* (members) can get season tickets. Television broadcasting deals are negotiated individually, and the star players will provide Real Madrid with an excellent bargaining chip. If the players bring on-the-pitch success, then there will be a positive impact on the Real Madrid brand, but if not the impact may be more tactical than in strategic brand building: *galácticos* may well enhance their own image rather than that of Real Madrid.

Yet if Reichheld's arguments about making the first step towards creating loyalty hold true (see Reichheld 1997), this type of strategy may still be effective. If Kaká moves from Real Madrid to another club, a proportion of fans will switch allegiance, but others originally attracted to support the club by their support for the player might, however, retain their interest in the club even after the player moves on. If they have built behavioral or even attitudinal loyalty to the club, they will remain as fans.

Image rights

"You're a marketer working in football, so explain image rights." This was one of the first challenges leveled at me when I began working in football. I still believe that image rights are largely about fixing the brand value of an individual in a contract, and so are as much legal as they are about brand value. Here, however, is my attempt to explain.

Chapter 1 establishes that football brands may be built around clubs, tournaments, football bodies, or individual players. One of the reasons fans might support a club is that they are attracted by the style of play or by the excellence of a particular player. So the player has a value to the club for which he or she plays. Image rights are contractual agreements about the extent to which a club can use the individual's name or image for its commercial gain, and how much the individual will be paid for this. When Kaká, Ronaldo, or David Beckham signs for a club, they will bring in money to that club through sale of replica shirts or from other products that bear the name or photograph of the player. Image rights are an agreement for an individual player to receive a percentage of proceeds from anything that bears their name or image. Image rights do not only happen in football and other sports, they are common in the entertainment industry, and might include such things as using Madonna's image to promote an album or George Clooney's for a film.

Image rights will usually only be for use of the image in relation to the club. Most often image rights agreements are not exclusive, but rights remain with the individual, who can also sign a series of deals, often through a PR or media company set up in the individual's name. As football is a team sport, commercial agreements will usually involve using the images of more than one player, so that one player does not get over-exposed. The agreement will also usually be that the higher-profile players will be seen alongside younger or lower-profile players so that the higher-profile players do not get to do all of the promotional work, or have their images used disproportionately.

Role of media

Political marketing talks about the way in which a politician's message can be distorted by external "noise" in the system. This might be intentional "spin" which is designed to make the politician or party appear in a more positive light. Alternatively, it might be distortion to the intended message or image that happens because of the way the media portray the message.

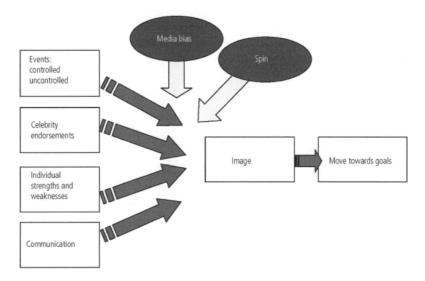

Figure 3.2 Possible distortions to marketing messages

The image that an individual portrays is a mix of:

- an individual's own personality and strengths and weaknesses
- the way in which this is communicated either by the individual or club
- outside events which may be outside the control of the individual or club
- celebrity endorsements.

Personality, and strengths and weaknesses

Whether or not an image is positive will be, at least partly, built on the characteristics and achievements of the individual. If an individual player has an excellent playing record and has been a hero in key matches, the values that are associated with the individual may be based on these successes. Other values with which individuals are associated will depend on the type of player, and the playing style. Stuart Pearce, for example, embodied a fighting spirit and never say die attitude as a player, which will continue to be associated with him as a manager. In some instances, however, values that are not so positive are associated with individual players. Sometimes this may be because the individual is introverted or uncomfortable being interviewed, so that the strengths of the individual are not recognized by fans.

Communication

This last point highlights the importance of effective communication. In the current high-profile game, clubs should take seriously the media or public speaking training of young players who may well be thrust into the spotlight. It is of benefit both to the player and club if they are able to communicate with press, fans, or commercial sponsors should the occasion arise. This will also help to improve the marketing attractiveness of these members of the squad, who might be exceptional players who could do with a little help with their communication skills.

Events

Individuals are sometimes perceived negatively because of particular episodes in their past. The "bad boy" reputation may sometimes be exaggerated by the media, but negatives often have some basis in a disciplinary record, off-the-pitch bad behavior, having played for a rival club, or simply having performed poorly for a period of time. Some of these negatives might be removed by self-development or minimized by positive behavior over a period of time. Other events might also enhance someone's image. A fringe player who scores a crucial goal will immediately be raised to the status of hero!

Endorsements

While well-paid endorsement opportunities are understandably attractive to players and agents, the advisability of deals depends on how well they fit with an individual and his values. So an endorsement opportunity for a low-calorie product may not be such a good idea for a player whose nutrition is not of the best, and who is often pictured leaving fast-food restaurants. Similarly, a prestige sports car may not be a great choice of endorsement for someone with several speeding penalties on their driver's license. It is useful to remember the big picture when evaluating whether or not to sign up to a deal.

Spin and media bias

The word "spin" was not originally used in its current meaning until around 1992. The origins of the term are in public relations surrounding politicians, although "spin" is now used to mean a whole set of marketing communication tools. Gilfeather (2002) highlights its use, for example, by the *Daily Mirror*, which described the government's advertising budget as being money that would be spent on "spin." During the 2004 US Democratic Convention, Schroeder (2004) describes how cameras kept cutting away from the speaker, ex-President Clinton, to show celebrity members of the audience. These included Richard Kind, an actor from *Spin City*, then an actor who plays a director of communications in the television series *The West Wing*. The clear inference was that a President under whose time in office the term "spin" gained in popularity was being shown alongside actors who are associated in the public's mind with "spin."

Andrews (2006) explains that the term "spin" has changed from a technical term for a technique used in political campaigning, to a general term for political campaigning, to a description of the media activities of governments, particularly in the United States and the United Kingdom, and now to a description of public relations as a whole. He ascribes this both to the employment of PR professionals, who are often nicknamed "spin doctors," and to tabloid "speak," which uses particular names for certain types of activity.

Spin is one of two types of distortion that can alter the message that is sent out about "image." This refers to the process where a message is given or portrayed in a certain way for PR reasons. The second distortion may occur as a result of media bias, in which certain areas of the media wish to show an individual in a positive or negative way.

In political marketing both of these are understandable. It is the PR professional's job to highlight positive aspects of the individual they represent to build that person's or the party's image. Media bias may occur because publications align themselves politically with different political parties, and will be inclined to favor those who share their views as opposed to those who do not.

In football and other celebrity worlds, bias may occur because of the relationship that an individual has with the press. A local media reporter told a story about two Premier League managers whose area he covers:

> I am a supporter of x's team but I can't bring myself to like him, he is arrogant to the press, doesn't turn up when he says he will, never gives a good story. The other one manages the rival team, but he is always pleasant, seems like a really nice guy and everyone gets on well with him. When results started to go against x's team, he started a real "charm offensive" but it was too late, no one was taken in by it.

It was no surprise that media jumped straight into speculation about whether the manager of Club x would be sacked. Perhaps they even contributed to his downfall, as fans read papers, and dissent built up a head of steam. Similarly, managers who have better relations with media may even receive supportive press comments when the going gets tough.

In portraying image, it should be remembered that everyone tries to show themselves in a positive light. If this is too inauthentic, people can see through it, and it will be considered as "spin." Ultimately this adds to the negative perception.

Football brands and communities

The friendships and common interests that develop among fans of a football club have prompted discussion of football communities. These may be local communities surrounding a club, but can also be broader, even global, communities of fans who define themselves by a shared passion.

The community to which a fan belongs is no longer always defined by where they live, but by which club they support. Chapter 2 discusses why fans identify with particular clubs. This chapter discusses the broader concept of football communities and the way in which football brands are pivotal in these.

Academic literature increasingly refers to communities of "like-minded individuals" who unite behind a common interest as being like some kind of "modern tribe." Coming from post-modern marketing, *modern tribes* are defined as being groups of individuals with shared interests, be it devotees of a particular type of music, a fashion, participants in a sport, or fans of a sports brand. This shared interest provides a sense of unity and belonging, which boosts the self-esteem of the group members (Cova 1997). The tribes are modern, rather than traditional, tribes because they are not bounded by geography but by a sense of belonging. For this reason, membership of a modern tribe offers a sense of identity, which can cut across differences in religion, beliefs, and social class. The value that this type of belonging and identification offers to individuals is seen by researchers like Cova (1997) and Maffessoli (1996) as being particularly important now in a society where people have lost many of those things that they used to believe in and value, such as religion, extended family, and local community.

The idea that football and other sports provide meaning for people with otherwise humdrum lives is not new. Football historically provided escapism for people, usually men, who worked hard in industrial communities. The origins of football are as a working-class game supported mainly by men who worked in hard jobs – mining, steel, manufacturing, and shipbuilding – and gained a release from this existence through playing and watching sport.

In the 19th century, the original members of the English Football League charged around 6d (pre-decimalization English pence) to attend a match. At that time a visit to the music hall or cinema was around half that price, and the matches were also on Saturdays, when many manual workers would be unable to get time off. Russell (1997) sees this as an attempt to position football to a certain social class, possibly to exclude poorer or rowdier elements of the crowd:

> In terms of social class, crowds at Football League matches were predominantly drawn from the skilled working and lower-middle classes …. Social groups below that level were largely excluded by the admission price.

At this stage, the role of football clubs went beyond a mere distraction. In his discussion of the history of football, Richard Holt (1989) describes football clubs as being the way in which fans, most often men, were taught how to behave. The heroes and football teams they supported were examples that reflected a spirit and behavior on which a community might model itself. Sport embodied teamwork, effort, and the idea of improving by practice, and its heroes were historically everyman figures drawn from the ranks of the communities in which they played.

Football clubs helped people in communities to work out what made them distinctive from another town, city, region, or country. This might explain why most fans want to believe that they are the most passionate, loyal, fanatical, or resilient, because these are values that reflect their own lives and feelings about their neighborhood.

More importantly, in the late 19th century, a time of rapid industrialization and urban development, Holt believes that football was important in creating identity as the workforce and population of these places was often in flux, and it might otherwise be difficult to create a sense of cohesion and belonging.

This idea is perhaps truer than ever in today's society, as Cova (1997) and others argue that people have lost many of the traditional "organizations" that dictated the rules and provided a set of values and yardsticks for how to behave. In Robert Bolt's play *A Man For All Seasons* (first staged in 1960), the confusion and lack of direction that exist in a society without rules are beautifully expressed by Sir Thomas More's discussion of what would happen if all the laws in the country, depicted as hedges with which the country is planted, were "cut down." Without these "hedges," a wind would blow, which would make it hard for people to stand upright.

Without hedges, or rules, to guide people in ways of behaving, societies become anarchic and chaotic. Football "tribes" or communities are not traditional groupings, but they do provide a set of beliefs and behavior that helps group members to define who they are and how they should conduct themselves. So football communities help to fill a void in society.

The nature of what the fans do to earn a living may have changed, but the value offered by football to communities has not. In part, football may be about escapism. An exciting match can help people to rise above their daily problems and challenges. There is a feel-good feeling when the team wins. Bob Murray, former chairman of Sunderland AFC, explained to me once that the whole city got a boost when the team won. Bill Shankly famously said, "Some people think football is a matter of life and death. I assure you it's much more serious than that."

Belonging to a community of football fans offers something to the people in the group. Common support of a team is the glue holding otherwise diverse individuals together. Support of the club goes beyond support for individual players. Fans may have a favorite player and be devastated when they leave, but most fans will maintain their allegiance to a replacement player because they play in the team's colors.

Cova (1997) argues that what is important is not even the "thing" in which the group believes or is interested. The link between people is what matters. The common purpose, the values, rules, even the outward display of belonging such as team colors, learning communal songs, sharing travel or experiences with others who also belong to the group, replace the traditional communities and guidelines which society has lost. "Thus to satisfy their desire for communion, consumers seek products and services less for their use value than for what is called their 'linking value'" (Cova 1997: 67).

Modern tribes have been found among rappers and in-line roller skaters. One French researcher, Bromberger (1998), has even argued that football hooligans may be some kind of "warrior" tribe. Groups such as skinheads, mods, and teddy boys may have had similar motivation. The same type of "ritualized identification" with football is picked out by studies of football and society:

It could be argued that recent developments in and around football have seen this process emphasized with renewed vigor. Football clubs now, as much as ever, embody many of the collective symbols, identifications and processes of connectivity which have long been associated with the notion of community.

(Brown, Crabbe, and Mellor 2009: 303)

It is even argued that football fan communities are more like traditional than modern tribes, as there is a strong link between clubs and their communities in a geographic sense. Relocating teams, as in the case of MK Dons, can be met with a negative response from fans who believe that the team loses its meaning.

Overall, the concept of "community" and the way in which groups form around football clubs, remains the subject of debate (Brown et al. 2009). A set of important features of football communities recurs throughout these discussions:

- The groups appear to satisfy a need for *social bonding* (Cova 1997). Football can unite or divide family groups. Socially a busy family may come together to attend a match or be united in its shared support. Conversely, rivalries may exist where families support different teams. Friendships may also form through shared football support with fellow fans and members of a football web board, which can then extend to life outside football. There are numerous examples of people who have never met in person coming together virtually to support fellow fans in times of hardship and illness, where family tragedies and bereavements are mourned by the whole community while joyous moments, such as birth (of a new little fan), are celebrated by the whole group.
- They fulfill a *symbolic role* (Maffesoli 1996) for their community groups who engage in rituals that define belonging to the group (Cohen 1985). This might involve wearing particular colors, singing particular songs during matches, drinking in particular places before a match, liking or disliking particular players or indeed watching televised coverage of matches in particular locations – in the case of fans who form supporters groups in different geographic locations. In contrast, some symbolic belonging might involve fans showing support for the football team identified with a particular geographic place

just so that they can show support for that particular place, even if they are not particularly football fans.

- Turner (1969) argues in favor of *communitas*, a type of community where belonging even happens outside of, or in despite of, people's normal behavior. For a particular moment in time, groups of people come together in support of a particular team or sporting event regardless of religious, ethnic, or other differences that might usually divide them. Similarly fans of rival teams might unite in their respect for a charitable cause – such as Kick Racism out of Football – or in tribute to a respected individual, as in the joint tribute to Sir Bobby Robson by fans of Ipswich Town and Newcastle United. This type of intense connection is commented upon by Brown et al. (2009):

> We have observed many moments in which the "out-of-time social drama of a football match," be it watched live in the stadium or in groups in a public house, produces moments of intense group bonding and feelings of associated community. Within football stadiums [sic] it is undeniable that when goals are scored or other moments of high excitement occur, many "normal" intra-group rivalries and differences within fan communities are obliterated and a new form of community bonding temporarily emerges.

> How many usually restrained males shed tears with fellow fans or hug unknown strangers in the joy or sorrow of a football drama?

- Communities constantly reinvent themselves through good and bad times for football clubs. As the team prospers, is promoted and becomes more globally known, or if a team suffers a poor season and is relegated, some members of the community may join and others leave. These communities are entered by choice rather than pure geography, and their members tend to be enthusiastic and committed to the community.

Developments in fan ownership of football clubs might be expected to increase fans' identification with football brands. So Birkbeck's football governance reports show an increase in fan ownership as a result of initiatives such as Supporters Direct. In this case fans might join together to buy a shareholding in a club, perhaps to have a seat on the board. Recently fans of both Liverpool FC and Newcastle United have been involved in suggestions that fans might buy out the clubs and form a structure similar to that of Barcelona or Real Madrid.

Sport and cities

A number of areas of research look at the role of "modern cities" in society. The rapid urban expansion that followed the industrial expansion in the 18th and 19th centuries (Hughson 2009b) changed the geographic landscape of many areas. Lewis Mumford (1938) considers this type of city as both a "fact of nature" and a "conscious work of art." It is clear that sports stadia may also contribute to their physical environment both architecturally and by the contribution that sport makes to the local community.

Sport's contribution to the development of cities has not always been seen positively. Hughson (2009b) reflects on sports crowds in the United States at the turn of the 20th century, as being "associated with a 'mob' mentality. Boxing was particularly prone to crowd violence, but 'rowdyism' also occurred at baseball matches especially when fans believed that their team was on the wrong end of poor umpiring decisions." Riess (1991), however, describes the culture of support as being generally friendly so that fans could "sit in the stands together, argue about their heroes … and shake hands once the contest was over."

This friendly banter exists in some football cultures, but the rivalry is often very intense, and there can be deep-seated antagonism between rival fans. Sometimes this is linked to "local derbies," where rival town and cities are near neighbors. Rivalries may also exist within a city, as in the case of the different London clubs that are based in districts within the city, or between two clubs located in the same city. Examples of two-club cities include Milan, Rome, Glasgow, Manchester, Liverpool, and Birmingham.

Geography may exacerbate these rivalries. In countries such as England, the development of conurbations – compressed urban development, which makes one place merge into the next – means that rivalry between two separate towns or cities may now be replaced by suburbs where rival fans live side by side.

Some rivalries are essentially friendly: on Merseyside, families may be split between the "reds" of Liverpool and the "blues" of Everton, and fans may stand side by side at derby matches. Other rivalries may be heightened by religious divisions, such as that in Glasgow between the historically protestant Rangers, and the historically Roman Catholic Celtic clubs. Sometimes other local issues can compound sporting rivalries. Fans also look for reasons why their particular football rivalry is intense. For example, fans have described the rivalry between Portsmouth and Southampton as being linked to the fact that both cities were prominent shipbuilding centers, but the former focused on military and the latter on civil engineering. As a result of this specialization, Portsmouth was bombed more during the Second World War than Southampton. Similarly Sunderland was historically within County Durham and Newcastle within Northumberland in north-east England, and some fans draw upon historic conflicts between the two counties to explain why there is a "special" rivalry between fans of the two clubs.

Sporting success of football teams can result in civic pride and celebrations involving whole towns or cities, even those who are not particular supporters of the football team. In describing the development of football in particular locations, Russell (1997) even argues that particular sizes of town or city and link with urban growth were essential to the development of successful football brands:

> Dominance in football could belie the adage of "it's grim up north" in towns such as Preston and Blackburn and bring a swagger to their high streets. Indeed [football] developed free of the rural romanticism often associated with England sport, especially cricket. From its competitive inception in Britain, association football thrived in urban population belts and the size of town correlated with the prospect of success for its soccer team.

There is still a bias that means that football, and sport in general, is seen as "low culture" rather than the "high culture" which customers can get by visiting museums, theaters, concert halls, and art galleries. All the same, football is now an accepted part

of the culture of towns and cities. This is indicated by the number
of football exhibits in museums (Moore 1997) in Liverpool,
Glasgow, and indeed by Preston's National Football Museum.

Football stadia may add to the identity of the town or city in
which they are based. This could be because they have design
merit in themselves, as with the Munich Olympic Stadium, or
the Millennium Stadium in Cardiff, Wales. The latter can be seen
from anywhere in the city, and is a much more visible landmark
than earlier stadia in Cardiff. Sometimes the appeal of a stadium
lies in features that evoke memories of the past (Bale 1994). This
might, he says, lie in the use of a particular arch, although architectural replication does not necessarily mean that the features of
the stadium have to imitate early stadia to have an impact. Indeed
Bale thinks that "staged authenticity" detracts from real memories of the past and can be seen as pseudo. Hence he refers to
one US stadium, Oriole Park at Camden Yards baseball stadium
in Baltimore, as a "Disneyfied sportscape" because it replicates
old-style benches and arches to try to offer a nostalgic return to
former times.

Echoes of the past can be incorporated in less obvious ways, for
example in the use of names – Wembley Way remains at the new
Wembley although the "twin towers" of the former national football stadium in England are replaced by a distinctive arch, which
will become a new symbol for future generations. A number of
stadia retain parts of previous stadia in designated areas such as
their bars, even in their own museums and other areas, so that
fans can remember these although they are not part of the new
design.

New stadia are also shaped by historical football tragedies, such
as those at Heysel Stadium (Brussels, Belgium), Hillsborough
(Sheffield Wednesday's stadium in England) or Valley Parade
(Bradford City's football ground in England). These tragedies,
while they occurred for different reasons, have resulted in both
a lasting sadness and changes in legislation to ensure that they
can never happen again. The design of modern stadia in England
is influenced by the findings of Lord Taylor's report (Home
Office 1989), which led to upgrading of football stadia. Inglis
(1990) saw these upgrades as bringing to an end years of under-
investment and neglect of stadia. New stadia have tended,

however, to be functional bowls, and some argue that they lack the architectural appeal and heritage of earlier stadia.

In addition to the formation of new partnerships and the involvement of new stakeholders, new stadia and redevelopment may have significant benefits for the image of areas and cities.

These developments create income from local people who use the facilities. The location of a stadium and a successful sports team in an area may help to build the "image of a city as a lively and successful place" (Thornley 2002). The redevelopments that took place in Middlesbrough, Bolton, and Sunderland after new stadia were built are used as examples of British cities whose image of industrial decline has been altered to one of modern areas with new economic activity, often in "vibrant" sectors which stimulate the whole area.

Sometimes the image of a city is boosted by its involvement in hosting particular sporting events such as the Olympic Games or World Cup football tournaments. A successful host country bid will involve the use of a particular set of stadia in cities around that country. Bidders will market the city or town alongside the football venue, and benefits may be gained from both efforts, in economic terms from ticket and other revenue from the tournament, as well as by possible contributions to development of stadia and the surrounding area. The cities can also gain global publicity that may help to attract new businesses and tourism to the city and surrounding area.

Some of the examples used in this book are of football clubs as brands, but the concept of a brand is not restricted only to this type of organization. Some other types of organization – such as the football bodies and representative organizations such as the League Managers Association (LMA) – also have an "identity" or brand. (See Chapter 2, page 50, for a discussion of the LMA brand.) Other football initiatives relate to competitions. The UEFA Champions League has a brand: see Desbordes (2007) for Chadwick and Holt's discussion of the key success factors in building this global brand. They may also relate to a particular campaign or tournament, such as the 2006 FIFA World Cup in Germany.

The following case study talks about an example of this last type of brand, which has been developed to communicate the values that underlie Sunderland's bid to be a host city, should England be successful in its campaign to bring the 2018 or 2022 FIFA World Cup to England.

Case Study: Sunderland's 2018 or 2022 World Cup bid

The FIFA World Cup

The Fédération Internationale de Football Association (FIFA) World Cup is a men's football competition which runs every four years. The current format involves 32 teams competing in a tournament – known as the World Cup Finals – which lasts around one month. The qualifying phase for the World Cup Finals takes place over the three previous years. The successful teams, alongside the host nation, qualify for the final tournament. The World Cup is the most viewed sporting event in the world. The 2006 FIFA World Cup Final, which was held in Germany, attracted a global audience of 715.1 million people (www.FIFA.com).

The World Cup Finals comprise two stages: a group stage followed by a knockout stage. The group stage is made up of eight groups, each with four teams. Eight teams are seeded (including the host nation and others which are determined on the basis of FIFA world ranking and how well they have performed in recent World Cup competitions). Apart from these eight nations, teams are randomly assigned to groups. Since 1998, the draw has also been weighted to make sure that no group contains more than two European teams (as there are more teams that qualify from Europe than from other football federations).

The top two teams from each group advance to the knockout stage, in which teams play each other in one-off matches, which are decided by extra time and penalties if need be. The tournament culminates with quarter-finals, the semi-finals and the final.

The 2006 World Cup tournament, hosted in Germany, was the 21st tournament since the World Cup competition began in 1930. (Two tournaments were missed in 1942 and 1946 because of the Second World War.) From 1930 to 1970, the winners of the World Cup won the Jules Rimet Trophy (until 1946 this was known as the World Cup but it was renamed to honour the FIFA president who set up the first tournament). When Brazil won their third tournament in 1970, they were allowed to keep the trophy permanently. The replacement trophy, which is 36 cm high and made of solid gold, is awarded to the tournament winners until the next tournament, when it is passed on to the new winners and the previous winners are then given a gold-plated replica instead.

Deciding who hosts the FIFA World Cup

Given the popularity of the FIFA World Cup and the prestige of hosting the tournament, competition among potential host nations is fierce. In a process not dissimilar to that for the Olympic Games, nations put together joint or individual bids some two or three cycles ahead of the tournament that they wish to host. At the current time, decisions are being made about who should host the 2018 and 2022 FIFA World Cup Finals.

The location of early World Cups was decided by FIFA's governing board, but was the subject of some controversy among the countries competing for the cup. When the first World Cup was held in Uruguay in 1930, the length of the journey meant that only four European nations contested the cup. In 1938, FIFA's decision to hold the tournament in France provoked strong reactions from the Latin American nations, who had believed that the tournament would cycle between different continents.

Hence from 1958, the tournament alternated between the Americas and Europe. The increasing global appeal of the FIFA World Cup – and the increasing geographic scope of those qualifying for the final tournament – occasioned FIFA to hold the 2002 World Cup jointly in South Korea and Japan, the first World Cup Finals in Asia. In 2010 South Africa will become the first African nation to host the World Cup. As the 2014 World Cup is to be held in Brazil, this will also be the first time that two consecutive World Cups have been hosted outside Europe. The choice of host country is now determined by a vote among members of FIFA's Executive Committee. The rotation between continents in these last two cases was predetermined by FIFA, but the competition will be open to bidders from any continent for 2018 onwards.

The process of determining the host nation goes through a number of stages. First after initial expressions of interest a bidding nation receives a "hosting agreement" from FIFA to explain what would be expected of a strong hosting bid. At this stage, the national football association of the country is also expected to officially confirm its bid. On receipt of these official expressions, FIFA inspectors visit to determine that countries match the requirements of World Cup host countries and report back on the countries. Decisions on the host of both the 2018 and 2022 World Cups are to be announced at the same time.

England's 2018 World Cup bid

England last hosted the football World Cup tournament in 1966, a tournament engrained in English consciousness as the only time England have won the World Cup. There is no set agreement on geographic rotation of the tournament, as new potential markets bid to host the games in each cycle, as well as others from Europe, Asia, and Latin and North America.

At the current time it seems likely that the host for the 2018 tournament will come from Europe, Asia, or Oceania. In March 2009, 11 bids were submitted, from potential host countries including Australia, Mexico, Holland/Belgium, Spain, and China. Mexico withdrew its bid in September 2009. FIFA has indicated that it is not looking for joint bids (there were two such bids from Holland/Belgium and from Spain/Portugal). Major competition is expected to come from Australia, China, and Spain.

The 2018 bid is considered to be important to the development of future fans and for football in England. On the bid website, bid CEO Andy Anson explains:

> In just over a year's time, Fifa will make a decision that will touch a whole generation of football fans. The challenge for the next 13 months is to convince 24 Fifa Executive Committee members that England will be the perfect host of the World Cup in 2018.
>
> England is passionate about football, it is in our DNA. Thirty million people attend matches every year. Six million play football every week, almost a million of them female. Four

hundred thousand people volunteer to run local teams, leagues, or drive the team bus just to help out.

These fans come from all parts of our multicultural society. It is this diversity that will make England capable of offering an enthusiastic and knowledgeable home-from-home welcome to all visiting country's teams and fans. We are uniquely positioned to welcome the world to our doorstep.

Host cities

As part of a successful 2018 or 2022 World Cup bid by England, a number of towns and cities would be identified as venues for World Cup 2018 or 2022 matches. Being a successful bidder would mean qualifying matches during the World Cup finals were played in this location, and teams were accommodated in the surrounding area in the run-up and during the tournament. The cities bidding for inclusion as hosts for 2018 or 2022 included Birmingham, Bristol, Derby, Hull, Leeds, Leicester, Liverpool, London, Manchester, Milton Keynes, NewcastleGateshead, Nottingham, Plymouth, Portsmouth, Sheffield, and Sunderland.

Sunderland's 2018 or 2022 World Cup bid

To put forward their case as a potential host city, the different locations had to put together bids which explained why they would be good places to host a group in the first stages of the competition, and potentially also one-off matches in the knock-out stages of the tournament.

One such 2018/2022 bidding city is North-East England's largest city, Sunderland. If Sunderland are successful in their bid, World Cup matches will be played at Sunderland AFC's Stadium of Light in the event of England being chosen for the 2018 or 2022 World Cup tournament.

Sunderland's bid is very much a "team effort" involving a partnership between the City Council, Sunderland AFC, the businesses, schools, sporting facilities – in short, the people of Sunderland and the surrounding region.

On the England 2018 website, Sunderland's bid is described as having at its heart the longstanding cooperation between

Sunderland AFC and the City Council. The nature of the city and the region, with their excellent facilities and enthusiastic support for the bid, played a central role in the attractions of Sunderland as a host city.

In promoting their case, Sunderland embraced the whole of North-East England in its proposal, ensuring that as many places and people as possible across the region would benefit from playing a part in the biggest sporting event in the world.

The basis of its bid was that of involving the whole community – fans, schools, local businesses – not just those located in Sunderland but those in the surrounding area. Sunderland AFC and Sunderland City Council have teamed up to lead the bid for Sunderland, and the two organizations are working closely with partners across South Tyneside, County Durham, Tyneside, Teesside, and Carlisle. Among the venues to be used for visiting teams are Middlesbrough FC's Hurworth training facility and facilities at Darlington, Hartlepool, and Carlisle. This was a regional bid which drew on a broad base of support.

In launching Sunderland's 2018/2022 bid, Chairman of Sunderland AFC Niall Quinn called on local people to offer their full support to the bid:

> I've experienced first-hand the huge excitement a World Cup generates and it would be absolutely fantastic to see the Stadium of Light and the North East play a big part in such an international sporting phenomenon. I know that we've got what it takes to be a host city. The warmth and enthusiasm of the people are such assets for us and I ask everyone, young and old, to put their heart and soul into supporting our bid.

Sunderland Bid Champion, former Olympic athlete and lifelong Sunderland supporter, Steve Cram commented:

> The Football Association has made it clear that the level of public support each bidding city generates will be taken into account when the final list is chosen to form part of England's proposal to host the World Cup. The Sunderland campaign is going really well and tens of thousands of

people have backed the bid. However, we want even more names on our list, so that we can demonstrate just how passionate people are about bringing World Cup football to North East England. I urge fans to sign a book or log onto www.sunderland2018bid.com and show their support for this great bid.

The Sunderland 2018/2022 bid was submitted to the Football Association on 26 November 2009, with a decision on the final list of prospective host cities to be included in the England proposal due just over a month later. On December 16, 2009, the Football Association announced its decisions on which host cities would be included in the England 2018 or 2022 World Cup bid. Sunderland was delighted to receive confirmation that it was a successful bidder (BBC Website 16 December 2009 http://news.bbc.co.uk/sport1/hi/football/internationals/8414235.stm). A tireless 12-month campaign had seen the whole region get behind the bidding process, and the collaboration between the City Council and the football club, together with the enthusiastic support of the public, brought about the result that the bid team were hoping for.

In discussing the successful candidates –and the process of selection – Lord Mawhinney explained that bids were considered in terms not just of stadia, but of all the elements – such as travel, accommodation, and security – that might make up the criteria for a good host city. Sunderland's bid was one of those considered to represent the strongest combination of elements which would help England's bid to be as attractive as possible compared with rival bidders.

Sport and regeneration of communities

Research suggests a link between sport and urban development (Schimmel 2001). A number of recent football stadia developments have followed the US model of including urban regeneration, particularly affordable housing, in the schemes. Examples include Watford, Arsenal, Sunderland, and Manchester City, where creating a new stadium brings infrastructure improvements such as regeneration. The building of Arsenal's Emirates stadium in London meant redeveloping an underground station near the new stadium, and England's Wembley stadium meant major infrastructure improvements in the surrounding electricity and transport provision. New stadia are often built on brownfield or industrial sites, and the stadium is the focal point of broader regeneration initiatives in the whole area, as was the case in east Manchester with the City of Manchester stadium. This type of complex initiative may involve partnership between football clubs, local neighborhoods, and town or city councils, with regional and even national governmental agencies.

Where a stadium is built specifically for a particular event, such as the City of Manchester stadium, created for the Commonwealth Games in 2002, challenges for those involved in planning are community acceptance of the stadium and the way in which its image may shift when it moves from being a national icon to the home of a particular club. The response to Amsterdam Arena when it moved from being part of an Olympic bid to the stadium of football club Ajax indicates that this can be a difficult transition.

New football stadia are most often either on the edge of a city or in inner-city locations.

When stadia are built in inner cities, as in the case of Arsenal FC's new stadium, the Emirates, which is close to the location of the old ground, the land released from the old stadium may have resale value for housing. Arsenal's Highbury stadium pitch, which had fans' ashes scattered on it, was turned into a memorial garden, and the industrial site used for the new stadium has been redeveloped and will, it is hoped, generate employment and revenue so that it will be welcomed by people living in the area.

The French national football stadium (Stade de France) was built in a deprived Parisian suburb which needed to be regenerated. Given that it was a catalyst for broader regeneration, the hope is that it will be viewed positively by the community in which it is built (Newman and Tual 2002).

If, however, a stadium is built on the edge of a city, there may be advantages such as access to the ground and availability of space to build other facilities, but the stadium may suffer for not having a surrounding community. There is a danger that the facility might be under-utilized and not embraced by those who live in the nearby city.

Football and social responsibility

The concept of corporate social responsibility (CSR) is increasingly important in sport. There are a number of examples of community initiatives related to the Super Bowl in American football, in Welsh rugby as well as in football around the world. For example, rugby is considered to be a significant tool for "(re)imaging and (re)imagining" the Welsh national identity.

Sport is frequently suggested as a means of increasing social inclusion, and of engaging with a sometimes diverse population within a community. The Football Task Force (1999), the Independent Football Commission (2004), UEFA, and FIFA all highlight the potential impact which football can have in tackling a number of different social issues. These include:

- diverting young people from crime or anti-social behavior
- engaging young people in education, whether formally or informally
- promoting sporting activity and tackling rising problems with obesity
- encouraging social cohesion.

In 2007, however, Tacon suggested that there was as yet little evidence to show the level of impact that football is having on these issues. Such evidence would move the role of football in communities from being something that people believe is inherently good, to being able to evaluate and prioritize areas, and perhaps also to generate additional funding, on the basis of specific evidence of impact.

Discussions of sport and social inclusion in the early 1990s began to point to sport as being beneficial to communities. The Football Foundation funded Football and its Communities research (Brown, Crabbe, and Mellor 2006), which later developed the list of areas to include:

- developing "primary group" relationships

- health awareness and health education
- drug awareness and education
- giving opportunities to develop leadership skills
- study support and educational help for under-performing students
- social skills, self-esteem, and life skills
- leadership development
- help with developing family and community cohesion
- adult learning
- anti-discrimination work to educate and provide opportunities for excluded groups.

The programs that football clubs currently offer tend to focus on encouraging people to share values, which Mellor (2008) argues will, in turn, help to create a stronger civil society. They also provide skills that help people to enjoy better job opportunities and equal access to these opportunities.

Mellor defines this as the "third way" of tackling social exclusion. The "third way" is a term coined by Anthony Giddens (1998) based on shifts in US democratic thinking which identified key characteristics for political thinking in the current era.

Sport is classically seen as improving the sense of inclusion among communities, although there are arguments over whether the community spirit that comes from football and other sports is permanent, or linked only to the duration of particular sporting events. The identification that community members may have with sports and sporting heroes as unifying forces may add to the value of engagement between football clubs and their communities.

Football clubs play a special role because the values that fans associate with football and the shared identity it encourages fit closely with the agenda for third way policies. Hence the white paper *Our Towns and Our Cities: The future – Delivering an urban renaissance* (Department of Communities and Local Government, 2000) claims that sport should be used to tackle social exclusion because it builds "civic pride." Similarly the English Football Association comments on the benefits of the "sense of community empowerment" that football clubs can foster among groups who are typically excluded from mainstream society.

One worry is whether the same individuals who feel themselves to be excluded from society might likewise feel themselves to be excluded from involvement in football. This might be because of the cost of attending matches, or because of a sense that "football is not for the likes of me." Whilst the racism of the 1960s and 1970s is thankfully a thing of the past, the fan bases of many clubs still do not fully reflect the diversity of the communities in which they are based (Blackshaw 2008).

On the pitch, the activities of anti-racism groups, such as Kick Racism out of Football and Football Unites, Racism Divides, have helped football to make massive strides in the last 30 years. It is relatively easy for marketers to present images of unity and diverse fan bases, but this needs to be translated into the reality experienced by the diverse communities themselves.

A football fan will "self-identify," and reasons for non-attendance at matches (see the example of Asian British fans given below) sometimes include comments such as "I look at the crowd and they are mainly white and I do not feel as though I will fit in." This is not necessarily "real," but a perceived exclusion – indeed the crowd might be welcoming. Evidence on the uniting force of football fandom suggests that anyone who supports the team is welcome as part of the fan community, although some still argue that this may be as temporary as the duration of a particular sporting spectacle. Creating a real sense of inclusion and belonging is likely to require more frequent and sustained efforts by clubs to create opportunities for integration.

Asian British fans and football

The concept of community and support for football teams has its roots in broader societal issues. This case study looks at some of the issues that arise from discussion with Asian British members of communities in the Midlands and London areas of England about the reasons that they would, or would not, support football teams. The case is based on research conducted for the Football Association into whether or why Asian British fans would support the England national football team.

One of the first issues which arose in discussing the national team was whether fans perceived themselves to be British, or still had a stronger association with the country from which they, or their forebears, originated.

A large majority of second and third-generation Asian British identified themselves as being British, while also acknowledging and respecting their ethnic Asian origin. One of the participants from London discussed origin as follows: *"I really don't know what being British means to me. I'd say I'm from London, not from Britain. Rather than Britain I'd say England. I've rarely said to someone I'm British. Possibly English, more likely a Londoner."*

The issue of perceived identity was also influenced by education and the type of area in which the respondents had been brought up.

Differences could be seen among some of the individuals who had grown up in mainly, or solely, Asian neighborhoods compared with those from more mixed areas during the formative years of their childhood, *"Living in an all-Asian area, I went to an all-Asian school, even playing footy, all my mates were Indian but I liked it …. don't really bother me you know what I mean …. I love India stuff, music, food ….I have total respect for who I am!!!"* Discussions among participants in focus groups suggested, however, that those who had grown up in areas that were predominantly "white" or attended mixed-race schools were more like to identify with being British than those who lived in Asian communities: *"I was brought up in an all white area … so all my mates where white … and even when I went to school again it was a white area. So I suppose I do see myself as British because I was surrounded by people for whom this was just assumed."* The way in which individuals perceive themselves played an important role in levels of support for the England team, and also for interest in football more generally.

Some participants, who played football in mixed race teams as children, identified themselves as being British and said that they now felt no ethnic distinction from their white friends. One or two did perceive themselves to be different even though they had grown up playing football, *"When we were picking sides to play football, I always got picked last … because I'm Asian … well usually just before the fat guy …!"*

Despite these perceptions, it was unanimously felt that encouraging children to play football in racially diverse teams from a young age prevents the development of any ideas of ethnic distinction, not just in relation to football but as a means of integration into the local community. With all children, the need to fit in was perceived to be important. Focus groups suggested that football is subconsciously used as a tool to deal with the problems of peer pressure in a mixed-race community. Showing support for a team that your peer group cheers on helps to develop a sense of identity with the group. It serves as a common ground irrespective of race or ethnicity. This helped to decrease feelings of exclusion.

Influence of football in England on Asian British

When the discussion began with sports in general, it was found that football was the most popular sport amongst second and third-generation Asian British, in particular those between the ages of 15 and 25. Being the national sport of England as well as the most popular sport in the country, it draws the entire nation's attention. Interest was fuelled by the game's significance for the country, as a means to fit in with the culture, but also due to a growing love for the game. Being a part of the same country, Asian British people felt that they share similar interests to the white majority and have developed a similar emotion towards the game. In a heterogeneous society like England, sports and football in particular has the ability to integrate this mixed-race society. *"Footy is an English thing so I suppose sometimes to fit in you want to get in with it …. you know what I mean."* The second generation of Asian British people has developed a strong interest in the sport as a means of acculturation, but also because they have grown up in a country in which football for many is a way of life.

Influence of club/league football

The participants of the focus groups showed greater support for club or league football than for the England national team. Perceptions were that this is a common view among the Asian community. There seemed to be a deep sense of belonging and affiliation to clubs like Manchester United, Liverpool, Arsenal, and Chelsea, compared with the emotions projected for the English national football team, possibly because there is less concern about "Englishness" and an easier relationship with a local team. Analysis of the data reveals a repeated view that this is a result of being brought up in the same area as these clubs and developing a local pride, which results in a stronger association and belonging with a social group. Whilst local pride may partly explain patterns of support, some participants suggested a feeling that it was important to be a fan of "successful teams." Being a "football fan" was an expression that most Asian British people associated with white people. *"The Brits love footy you see ... and I feel to be part of it, all right, you need to support the right teams ... you get me ...?"* That way it is easier to be seen as a football fan. English Premier League football clubs were perceived as being more successful than the English national team. This was seen as a reason that successful English club sides have attracted most support in the Asian community.

Image of football in England

Despite the latent interest in football expressed by a majority of the Asian British, focus group participants felt that the image of football in England suffers from a lack of Asian representation in various areas.

Traditional football fan image

Asian British have a stereotypical image of football fans. Participants used pejorative words such as "skinhead," "fat," "thugs," "tattooed," "beer bellied," and "hooligans" to describe a football fan. Many participants felt that, being Asians, they didn't think they could relate to this image, and as a result felt excluded from being a part of the game. *"When I go to a game I see beer bellied, 30 to 40-year-old tattooed men, your new generation kind with bad haircuts, all spiked up, piercing, I wouldn't say everyone's like that, but basically you get to a game and the crowd's all white."*

Lack of Asian spectators at games

The participants in the research believed that ethnicity was a major reason for exclusion from football. They often reported feeling uncomfortable being spectators at a match, and felt unwelcome and out of place in the crowd of "white" fans while being inside or around the stadium or the game atmosphere. *"Every match I have been to I get bloody looks … like bloody hell get over it you know what I mean? For shame's name, I live in this country and I am British!"* This negative vibe seems to result from a sense of fear from still being a minority in the crowd.

"I haven't had any racial slurs thrown at me when I went to a game, but if I did … I'd never go back …. why should I have to deal with that sh••?" Participants did suggest that the "white" community makes them feel different because of the color of their skin. Participants revealed that white fans glared at them as if it was anomalous for them to be present at matches as they are "brown." (The use of the word "brown" to describe the Asian British respondents to this study was the respondents' own. The respondents said they were not black or white, and described themselves as "brown.")

Under-representation of Asian British people in football

Some felt that the lack of representation in other related areas of football, meant that the image of football was out of line with the multicultural society of England, and more specifically with Asian British, *"Never see representation on posters or leaflets to attract us … same typical white guy, not even a real role model … just some Joe Bloggs … so really how is that going to catch my attention?"* Despite this view, a majority was clear that they did not want to become "token representatives" and be included on a brochure or in advertisements just to suggest that football is achieving its social obligation towards the representation of ethnic minorities. *"An Asian on this leaflet is a real 'slap in the face' … who are they trying to fool? Unless this is 'real representation' and there is demonstrable participation of Asian British in management, coaching, spectators and players then it is a token gesture. You never see a single Indian player … or even a coach … and, you know what, that does need to change ....I don't understand why it hasn't already ... we live in the 21st century!"*

Lack of Asian player representation

Participants perceived that the lack of Asian British role models in football must be something to do with racism and stereotypical beliefs about the Asian British. There was a general lack of comprehension of the failure of any Asian British players to excel over such a long period. It was agreed that the presence of a Asian British player would not only increase their interest in football but also pull in the Asian crowds to watch matches at stadia, in this way increasing the support from the large Asian community. Again, this could not, however, be for the sake of "tokenism." *"I wouldn't want to see the token brown person in any area of football but a better and open representation of Asians in football would help the matter I suppose."* It was also felt that a successful Asian British player on the pitch would lead to an acceptance by the white football fans of the involvement of Asian British in football, making the transition of more Asian British into professional football easier. *"Having an Asian player would be the next step right, but they have to be good, right, can't be rubbish, we need to prove that we can be just as good."*

A majority of the participants said that seeing Asians in the team would encourage them to believe that as long as they show promise in the sport, they have a chance to make it as well. More importantly they felt it would lead to their families believing that Asians can make it big in professional football, and therefore encourage them to provide support for the development of their talent. That so few role models have emerged naturally over the last decades also prompted a discussion about why this was the case. Maybe Asians are just not physically built to be footballers? The participants believed that *"maybe Asians don't have the physical frame needed to be athletes,"* and joked about how *"Asians just aren't physically suited to play football."*

Lack of opportunity to develop talent

Another issue that emerged was a perceived lack of infrastructure and facilities for the development of the talent of Asian British.

Participants felt that, unless Asians were provided with the appropriate support to nurture their skills within various areas of the game, they would not be able to compete at the levels required to be in professional football. Suggestions to increase participation included support through community development by providing funds for causes such as the upgrading of parks or football grounds, setting up clubs or little leagues in Asian-dominated areas, and affordable enrolment fees to participate at a higher level in mixed-race clubs or leagues.

Lack of parental support

All the participants in the research shared the same opinion on the lack of professional Asian football players and its influence on their scope in football. Most asserted that Asian parents would not approve of or support football as a career choice for their children, as they believed to do so was taking chances with their future. *"Asian parents don't usually see being good at a sport as anything extraordinary, they don't understand the social aspects of playing a sport, they would rather that you study and do well in school and at your academics."* Children were encouraged by parents (that is, the first-generation immigrants) to pursue more traditionally rewarding careers like law, medicine, or engineering, which guaranteed them some financial stability. *"My parents want me to do good in life … .so becoming a doctor is more realistic, you get me … plus more money and guaranteed to do well … whereas playing footy they think, no chance!"* However, the discussion revealed that children who showed promise in sports such as cricket or tennis were encouraged and supported by their parents. It seemed that this could be attributed to the existence of successful Asian role models in these sports. *"To make money in football, you gotta be right there at the top, I don't see any Asians being up there, I don't want to risk my future … you get me? The idea of playing pro football is a pure gamble! Tennis or cricket … yeah maybe, it looks like the chances of success are higher, I see people like me who have made it!"*

It was generally considered that Asian parents view participation in football games as a fun activity rather than even recreational exercise. Young Asians are encouraged instead to concentrate on their studies. Another issue here is that gifted footballers are asked to commit themselves to academies at a very early age, and a large proportion drop out before reaching professional contracts. For any parent whose child might otherwise do better academically, there is a conflict between supporting a progression in football and other sports for which commitment comes at a later age. With no support from their parents to play on local teams and pressure to study, these young Asian British are left with no or very little time to improve their football skills, at an age when it is imperative for the development of their talent. This impedes any opportunity to play football at a higher level at a later stage.

High prices of tickets

Research further revealed that another deterrent to Asian British watching games at stadiums is the high price of football tickets. *"How many Asians do you know who are going to spend £40 to watch the game and then a minimum £20 to get there and to eat, drink another £20, so £100 to watch the game, now that's expensive!"* Football is often not seen as a family outing in Asian families, as the first generation has no interest in the sport, and so it is only the individuals of the second and third generation who are keen to go to watch a game at the stadium. Participants suggested that their families would not do so on a regular basis, but might do so on a one-off basis. To do so means spending a large amount of money on football as a recreational activity. It is either unaffordable or perhaps just not considered a worthwhile expense by Asian British.

Cricket versus football?

Throughout the research the Asian British showed a predisposition towards success. The 1980s Asian generation often started supporting Liverpool as a football team if they were football fans, because Liverpool were the most successful team of the time. *"I have always supported Liverpool ... they were the winning team back in my day and they still are .... I suppose. I guess Asians can be quite the glory hunters."* By doing this, they believed they were projecting the correct social image, and this would help them fit into society. This phenomenon can also be seen in cricket. When discussions turned to cricket and which national team to support, that is, either India/Pakistan or England, the participants felt they would support England at football irrespective of whom they played against, probably because none of the other options were as good. But when it came down to cricket they preferred to support either India or Pakistan, depending on their ethnic origin. The argumentation went, *"Cricket is the one sport at which India and Pakistan are successful, and Asians feel proud of supporting them."* The England cricket team is seen as being rather unsuccessful up until recently. *"It's the one thing the country is good at, for India or Pakistan it comes down to cricket so we support 'em, but with England it's football all the way!"* The only situation in which these participants would support England in cricket is when the country of ethnic origin is not playing (secondary choice). *"Cricket is different to footy ....India are good ...? So course I'm going to support them."* But research showed that most participants, namely the second and third generation of Asian British (between the ages of 15 and 25) and some between the ages 25 to 35 supported the England national team at football. Worryingly the younger age group (7 to 14) often preferred to support Brazil, *"Why would I want to support England at football, they're no good .... Brazil are much better."* To a suggestion that support might be on the grounds of local pride, these third or even fourth-generation kids were clear, *"We're not English, we're Indian."*

The next generation does, however, have allegiance to Premier League football sides.

(With thanks for their help in preparing this case study to Basheera Indorewala, Rinku Grewal and Bani Mehta.)

CHAPTER 4

Football brand experiences

This chapter begins by debating the types of experience offered by football, and how these might be enhanced to offer and vary the types of experience to maximum effect. It concludes by taking each of Pine and Gilmore's six challenges for experiential branding, and discussing how these might be applied to enhance the experience of engaging with a football brand.

What is a brand experience?

One of the rising areas of branding and services marketing is experiential marketing. Brand or service experiences are those that engage customers in memorable ways and coordinate the marketing offer to "perform" a marketing experience.

The concept of brand experiences was proposed in 1999 by Pine and Gilmore, who argue that experiential offerings have grown more rapidly than have commodities, products, or services over a comparable period of time.

An important distinction between brand experiences and other communication of brand values is that customers are encouraged to interact with the brand at various points during the experience. Moreover they are assumed to be active participants in the consumption of the brand, rather than passive recipients of information about the brand. Services marketing calls each contact between customer and service provider a "moment of truth" in which the customer judges whether the service or experience is consistent with what they expect (Bitran, Ferrer, and Oliviera 2008).

The creation of brand or service "experiences" can create an "emotional connection through engaging, compelling and consistent context" (Pullman and Gross 2004). Indeed authors have described us as living in a "dream society" (Jensen 1999), or an emotion economy (Gobé and Zyman 2001), in which marketers try to raise their services beyond commodities by creating an emotional attachment to them. To do this, marketers must work out what motivates fans to form attachment to football brands (see Chapter 2), then use their imagination to design the marketing offer in ways that will stimulate this attachment to the club.

When brand or service experiences have been analyzed – their benefits are frequently discussed in relation to other fields of entertainment, such as theater or VIP tents at sporting and other venues – customers are found to find a number of aspects important (Pullman and Gross 2004). These include both *physical* and *relational* elements of the service.

The physical elements include the sights, smells, sounds, and textures generated by tangible elements of the service. On an airline, the physical elements might include the size and comfort of seats, cleanliness, choice of meals, and use of menu cards or other "clues" to indicate the style of service. The physical dimensions of football brands include the stadia (see Chapter 3 and Chapter 4, page 122), catering, pre-match and post-match entertainment, as well as the match and team themselves.

The relational aspects of brand experiences are those that help to "meet or exceed people's emotional needs and expectations in addition to functional expectations" (Berry, Carbone, and Haeckel 2002).

Pine and Gilmore's brand experience framework

One of the founding works in the brand experiences field is that of Pine and Gilmore (1999). The framework is made up of two dimensions on which brand experiences can vary. These are:

- **Passive to active:** Does the customer interact with the brand or experience, or sit back and receive information about it?
- **Sensory intensity:** The customer may experience the service close up (immersion) or at a greater distance (absorption).

There is no value judgment about which end of the scale is better for either of these dimensions. In fact, in his discussion of the

Pine and Gilmore framework in relation to arts marketing, Petkus (2004) suggests that varying the distance at different stages of the experience might be optimal because too much distance can result in boredom, and too much close experience in burnout.

The richness of the experience, then, is a function of building in all four of the dimensions. Pine and Gilmore refer to a "sweet spot" which lies at the center of the four realms of experience. This does not mean that every experience should be between each of the dimensions, but that the overall experience might offer a balance of all of the four realms to achieve maximum effect.

The authors identify four *realms* of experience:

Absorption

- **Entertainment.** This involves passive participation in an event, where the customer simply takes in the experience, such as at a cinema. SENSING
- **Education.** The customer actively participates in this process by acquiring or increasing skills and knowledge. LEARNING

Immersion

- **Escapist.** The customer is immersed in the experience and actively participates in the experience. DOING
- **Aesthetic.** The customer is immersed and experiences closer and more intense stimulation of the senses than in entertainment, but is still passive rather than active. BEING.

Designing a brand experience in football

This section begins by discussing both the physical and relational features of a football brand experience.

Services marketing theory has long focused on the tangible elements of service design. For example, the physical surroundings of the service affect the way customers perceive the quality of a service. Wakefield and Blodgett (1996) suggest that sports venues are ideal for the creation of "servicescapes" that reinforce brand experiences because, unlike some other types of service, the fan spends a fairly lengthy time in the stadium. Contrast the challenges facing banks, fast-food restaurants, and a stadium in which fans spend several hours every home match during a season, and the opportunities are clear. When customers do not spend long in a particular place, they may notice more the intangible aspects of the service such as politeness of staff. When they are in the environment for lengthy periods, they also notice their physical surroundings.

The football servicescape

In a football context, the physical environment is closely related to the stadium and its facilities, although it might also include parking, travel, and other related parts of the service. Several customer surveys undertaken by football clubs reveal fans' concern about how easy it is to park, congestion on surrounding roads before and after matches, and the convenience and price of park and ride and other travel schemes. Another frequent theme is the length of queues at catering outlets, particular in older stadia, which may have relatively few outlets.

The football stadium could offer similar benefits to those described in services marketing and brand experiences, as it provides the ideal venue for the "sensual and psychological benefits" (Collier 1994) that contribute to the brand experience. Collier describes the physical benefits that could be offered by surroundings as including sights, smells, sounds, and feelings of status, privacy, or security. The sensual aspects of football brand experiences are described on page 125, which outlines how Pine and Gilmore's framework might be applied to football.

First, however, this section begins with a consideration of the broader physical surroundings of the football stadium, and the way in which this contributes to the fans' experience.

Physical surroundings

Physical surroundings are not only important with regard to safety and comfort, research also highlights the role that they can play in enhancing enjoyment and stimulation, and in adding to the pleasure of the experience (Mehrabian and Russell 1974). Bitner (1992) referred to these physical surroundings as the "servicescape." This servicescape plays an important role in customers' behavior, whether they want to spend more or less time in a place, whether they want to go back again, and how much money they spend while there. Bitner splits the servicescape into three parts:

- **ambient conditions:** weather, temperature, noise, music, smells
- **spatial layout:** the way in which the facility is laid out and how well it fulfils its purpose
- **signs, symbols and artifacts:** décor and other means of communicating and enhancing the image or mood.

In a sporting context, Wakefield and Blodgett (1996) identify five dimensions:

- layout accessibility
- facility aesthetics
- seating comfort
- electronic equipment and displays
- cleanliness.

Layout accessibility

This mainly relates to functional parts of the stadium, such as access to and exit from the stadia, access to catering and toilet facilities, shops and other parts of the stadia, which can enhance or detract from the experience. Issues of layout may go beyond the functional. There are good examples of the servicescape being designed in ways that are interesting and communicate a theme in theme parks, such as Disney World, and research shows that customers are likely to evaluate queues as shorter if they are entertained during the wait for the primary service.

Facility aesthetics

These relate to the architecture and interior design of a stadium. Increasingly stadia fulfill other roles, such as entertainment and leisure, at times other than match day, and an interesting and attractive venue is more likely to draw fans to use it at other times and for other purposes. In other forms of entertainment, customers often look at pictures of the venue on the Internet or go to visit it to decide whether it is appropriate for their conference, function, or other leisure activities. While a number of features will influence this decision, uncolored and dull walls, flooring, and functional bowl-shaped stadia miss opportunities to appeal to fans through use of color, memorabilia, and other artifacts.

Seating comfort

Decisions clubs make on when to replace old or worn seats, padded or plastic seats, the amount of space between seats and between rows, influence how cramped a fan feels. Also, some fans tend to stand up at exciting points, and once they do so everyone else also needs to stand up in order to see. Research into crowding (Hui and Bateson 1991) suggests that these aspects can all detract from the experience.

Electronic equipment and displays

While technology has moved on, the way in which clubs deliver information does not always make full use of the range of possibilities. Sometimes for financial reasons, data provision and scoreboards may not be high on the priority list for clubs, but there are far greater possibilities to engage with fans than are used. The way in which information is presented can even detract from the match. It is now commonplace to tell fans who scored a goal, the time of the goal, and so on. Occasionally clubs have older-style clocks (even those that count down from 90 minutes, which is no good for the nerves in tense matches!), or do not relay information other than the time. In sports settings now, graphics can be used to build excitement, and provide half-time entertainment such as trivia quizzes or instant replays, as well as simply noting time and score.

Cleanliness

Customers associate cleanliness with the quality of service. Both pre- and post-event cleaning are important in making sure that the venue is an attractive place to spend time, but Wakefield and Blodgett (1996) also note the importance of continuous cleaning to make sure the experience is not negatively affected by spilt drinks, rubbish, or unclean toilets.

In addition to the elements identified by Wakefield and Blodgett, other researchers have also pointed to the importance of catering and the overall atmosphere.

Catering

This includes not only the quality and price of food, but in the corporate rather than fast-food settings, the way in which it is laid out and presented. For the catering outlets, the challenges may be similar to those faced by fast-food restaurants, which must polish the service process to produce food of a consistent quality. This may sound simple but there have been high-profile difficulties when beer-cooling systems have failed or ovens ceased to work, or queues became too lengthy for the short half-time interval.

Overall atmosphere

The overall atmosphere of the stadium includes music, lighting, and use of colors (Baker and Cameron 1996). These aspects are discussed under football brand experiences, but include singing particular songs associated with the club and other, often unique, characteristics of the experience which can help to intensify the experience for fans.

Football brand experiences

Pine and Gilmore (1999) suggest that all of the physical elements should be consistent with a theme that is "concise, compelling and engages all senses with its interior design, employee dress and behaviour." How many concrete concourses remain in football? I have experienced many, especially in the away end of stadia, when a more congenial football theme could enhance the experience. In home areas, such a theme might make use of team colors and stirring images; in the away fans area, this might use a generic football legend theme. It is surprising how many home sections of stadia do not fully utilize the possibilities to think of the total experience of attending a football match.

Pine and Gilmore (1999) identify six challenges in designing a brand experience. These are:

- developing a cohesive theme
- forming impressions
- eliminating distractions
- providing memorabilia
- ensuring all senses are engaged
- gaining feedback to refine and improve the experience.

The challenges do not have to happen in a particular order, so a marketer might, for example, begin with thinking of ways to engage senses and make customers form impressions, then develop a theme.

Football and other sports naturally involve fans in experiences – a match lasts for a period of time and will involve highs and lows, intense drama and more relaxed periods. Fans might respond to what they see, the sounds of a ball being kicked, or the crowd noise.

Football marketers might think, however, about how they can build upon these experiences to engage to maximum effect with their customers. So for example, it might seem difficult to think about smells associated with football, and yet nostalgic memories might include the smell of liniment, or the smell of the match-day Bovril and pies. Touch might involve the old wooden seats, metal barriers on terraces or the turf. Taste might be the types of foods that fans eat, or used to eat, when they attend football matches.

Finding the sweet spot for football brand experiences

Passive or active?

There is considerable debate about the impact of seating versus terracing in football. The safety benefits of seating over standing are clear: it is not possible to over-congest an area of numbered seats, and seated customers cannot push or crowd others.

Yet at the same time, sitting is more passive than standing. It encourages customers to be less involved as consumers of the experience. It is no accident that at moments of high drama, fans are tempted to leap to their feet and be active, just as a manager on the touchline might pace up and down, shouting and gesticulating at the players, even though the extent to which this has an effect or is intelligible to the players is unclear. It is very hard to remain passive during a match, but the types of activity that it is possible to create during a match are restricted by the legislation and physical surroundings of the football stadium. Or are they?

There are numerous examples of activities, sometimes before a match or during the half-time interval, that are designed to engage fans in being active. The fan might be asked to enter competitions, sing, hold up a particular sheet of paper, or wear a t-shirt on the seat as part of a stadium-wide image or symbol. Pre-match entertainment and interval catering may involve fans in moving from their seats to other areas that are less constrained. While activity in football matches is limited, there are still possibilities for creating active parts of the football brand experience.

Close or distant?

A football match will naturally vary between the two depending on the intensity of the action during a match. As suggested by Wakefield and Blodgett (1996), intensity can be enhanced by replays, announcements, music, and the use of electronic scoreboards to reinforce goals and other key moments. Pre- and post-match will be different types of entertainment with a different level of intensity, but fans can still be engaged in the experience with competitions, multimedia, and creation of interesting physical surroundings which engage the senses in a less intense way than match action.

The four types of experience for football brands

Absorption

- **Educational (learning):** Clubs can create opportunities for fans to discover more about the club history, football characters, and past matches. The might do this in a multimedia way, and utilize material already available on the club website as talking points for fans. This dimension of the club's activities extends beyond match day and the stadium to involve the community activities of the club, and to associate it with educational opportunities more broadly.
- **Entertainment (sensing):** Pine and Gilmore describe this as

a process in which customers sit back and simply take in the experience, as they would, for example, in a cinema. Use of interviews, coverage of scores, or team footage on multimedia screens in the stadium and concourse offers many opportunities to use this more laid-back experience in-between the live match action.

Immersion

- **Aesthetic (being):** A number of clubs have created excellent bars, members' bars, or museum areas within the stadium. These combine memorabilia, match coverage, even architectural features from previous stadia to build the atmosphere for fans.
- **Escapist (doing):** Pine and Gilmore describe this as doing, when the customer is close to the experience and actively participating. This is probably the state of most fans during the intensity of a match when they are not only watching, but also encouraging, singing, or discussing the action with fellow fans. There is no need to create any more "escapist" experiences, but more to enhance the experience by interspersing the total match experience with the other types of experience.

Developing a cohesive theme

The theme of a brand experience should be unique and focused so that the impression given is that of a "single voice." For a football brand experience, the theme is clearly football, but different clubs might have a distinctive set of images and meanings which bring to life the particular experience of attending their match.

Each club will have particular players who embody a spirit, evoke a period in the club's history, or help to recall a famous victory. It will have a set of colors which will help to create a particular theme, the sound of its crowd might be distinctive, the ground may be architecturally unique, the football brand is located in a region, city, or town, and there may be famous images of the location which have a meaning to fans which goes beyond sport.

Forming impressions

First impressions are created by the ease of travel, parking, length of queues, and the helpfulness of ticket and stewarding staff. It may also be enhanced, however, by the club taking opportunities to provide excellent pre-match entertainment that engages with fans. Clubs can also reinforce what the club is about with use of history, images, and colors. For different parts of the service offer, this might range from how the concourse is decorated, themes of catering outlets, or the use of past players as ambassadors to host corporate guests.

Eliminating distractions

Experiences are improved by eliminating anything that does not fit with the experience or theme. Queues at catering, poor-quality food, warm beer, unhelpful ticket sales staff, seats with restricted views, over-zealous stewarding, or someone standing in front of you can all form this type of negative cue. These aspects are covered in more detail in the earlier discussion of the servicescape (see page 121). Pine and Gilmore (1999) refer to this stage as "eliminating negative cues." Once the club has spent time and effort in creating a positive experience, it is worth making sure that there is nothing that will detract from the overall enjoyment of the experience.

Providing memorabilia

As symbols and history are particularly important in developing football brands, they are also a key part of creating football brand experiences. Football abounds with opportunities to recall past triumphs, but there are also many lost opportunities among clubs that do not build on their history and bring to life a brand experience at relatively low cost by use of team colors, symbols, or enlarged pictures printed on the walls.

Ensuring all senses are engaged

While sport is essentially visual, there are also sounds, smells, and even particular materials that fans associate with football matches and their chosen clubs. When old stadia close, fans may bid at auction for pieces of turf, the seat that they sat on, or the barrier they leaned against. The importance that fans attach to these familiar objects, even to bricks and parts of stadia, suggest the range of possibilities for creating multi-sensory experiences around match attendance and support of clubs. Even for fans who cannot physically attend matches, technology allows for audio-visual experiences and for engagement and interaction with fans so that they are actively engaging with the club, its players, and becoming engaged with the brand.

Getting feedback to refine and improve the experience

How well do feedback mechanisms work? Does the club regularly ask fans what parts of the experience of being a fan they value, and what detracts from the experience? While marketers in organizations and clubs may spend large sums on communicating a set of values to customers, they do not always check whether the message that is received is the one intended. There may be gaps between the intended message and how it is interpreted. Sometimes a club may think it is communicating a set of values, but what is understood is totally different. Without feedback, there is no possibility of changing or tweaking a marketing offer. It may be that something good should be expanded, or that simple actions, or training, could remove a negative cue.

CHAPTER 5

Globalization of football brands

Introduction

This chapter looks at the globalization of the world in which football clubs operate. The chapter begins by looking at what globalization is, and what drives it to happen. It then looks at the drive to globalize brands in any sector, and what organizations might gain by doing this. The chapter then looks at the way in which globalization of markets and of brands affects football.

What is globalization?

The pace of globalization of the world economy has been intensified by a number of factors including the following.

Global competition

Even if a firm does not wish to internationalize – or thinks of itself in national or local terms – it may be competing against firms that operate on an international or global scale. These international firms benefit from spreading the risk of downturn in one market against other more buoyant markets.

- **Economies of scale.** International firms may also produce greater volumes of products, or offset the costs of their marketing across a larger global audience than is possible if they just serve one market. These economies (of scale) mean that they can undercut firms that work on a domestic basis.
- **Creation of free trade agreements.** Agreements such as those among members of the European Union (EU), or the

North American Free Trade Agreement (NAFTA) which spans the United States, Canada, and Mexico, mean that goods and services are traded more freely among members of these economic and political unions. These unions may also impose regulations – such as the Bosman ruling for European football players – which mean that firms have to think outside their own market to gain a full picture of the world in which they operate.

- **Liberalization of previously blocked markets.** Looking at a world map, it has historically been difficult to do business in some countries. In East and Central Europe prior to the 1990s, for example, trade had to go through the central Soviet structure rather than firms setting up individual deals. The percentage investment that foreign firms could have has also been limited at some stages in markets such as India and China.

   Market liberalization has made it possible to strike deals, use the Internet to get access to customers or to play football matches, broadcast or otherwise gain fans, and create a set of new international opportunities for firms in all sectors, including football brands.

- **Advances in travel and communication technology.** There is virtually nowhere in the world which is more than a day's travel away, and low-cost, or even free, communication is possible at the push of a telephone button or by using the Internet. Advances in travel and communication technology have shrunk the world for consumers who might import cars from other countries, buy books and CDs from around the world, and deal daily with call centers in remote locations without even being fully aware of the distances involved.

Convergence of consumer tastes

The advances in travel and technology, and the increasingly cosmopolitan consumer tastes that have resulted, mean that some research suggests that customers are increasingly similar in their tastes. The concept of the "global village" (Levitt 1983, Ohmae 1985) or borderless world, has prompted marketers to look at whether they can serve the world as one market, or a smaller number of markets, rather than having a different marketing strategy for every country or segment:

> Whether to globalize, and how to globalize, have become two of the most burning strategy issues for managers around the world. Many forces are driving companies around the world to globalize by expanding their participation in foreign markets. Almost every product market in the major world economies – computers, fast food, nuts and bolts – has foreign competitors. Trade barriers are also falling.
>
> (Yip 1989)

It is largely accepted that effective marketing must now be global in its understanding of the market in which a firm operates. Ohmae (1985), Yip (1989), and others present compelling arguments that the future lies in a global scope of operation. Only by operating across trading blocks can firms protect themselves against down-turns in a globally interlinked economy (Ohmae 1985). Only by maximizing sales in global markets can firms offset the increasing costs of remaining innovative (Lorenz 1985). If a firm does not operate globally it may be vulnerable to the actions of global competitors with greater resources and ability to direct these to gaining market share in any specific country (Hout, Porter and Rudden 1985; Hamel and Prahalad 1985). Based on this evidence, few would argue against the concept that firms are increasingly driven to globalize their scope of operation:

> Walk into a capital goods factory anywhere in the developed world, and you will find the same welding machines, the same robots, the same machine tools. When information flows with relative freedom, the old geographic barriers become irrelevant. Global needs lead to global products. For managers, this universal flow of information puts a high premium on learning how to build the strategies and the organizations capable of meeting the requirements of a borderless world.
>
> (Ohmae 1985)

The question for international marketing managers, then, is how to develop effective strategies for a global economy.

The importance of global brands

As globalization continues across all sectors, the brands that marketers use to encapsulate their product and service offers must be made available to customers internationally or even globally. Marketing literature has had a longstanding debate over the extent to which international marketers should standardize their marketing offer.

Multi-domestic marketers (those that have multiple marketing strategies for different markets), such as Nestlé and Unilever, were historically just as successful as those that branded in a standardized global way, such as Coca-Cola and McDonald's. Nonetheless there have been increasing arguments over recent decades over the value of global brands. Indeed even traditionally multi-domestic marketers have tended to standardize some of their brand offerings – such as Nestlé's KitKat and Nescafé brands, and Unilever's standardization of the brand names Jif (detergent) and Oil of Ulay to Cif and Oil of Olay respectively – and to launch new brands that appeal across more than just a single market.

Global marketing research provides arguments both for and against global standardization of the marketing offer. Arguments *for* standardization include:

- **Significant cost savings.** Although marketing argues in favor of offering products and services adapted to local tastes, revenue and profitability depend on both sales and costs. Offering the same basic product or service (maybe with some variation in features or usage) and coordinating marketing efforts behind a single brand can significantly reduce costs. Buzzell (1968) comments that "For some of the major packaged goods manufacturers, the production of artwork, films and other advertising materials costs millions of dollars annually. Although differences in language limit the degree of standardization that can be imposed, some common elements can often be used."
- **Consistency of marketing strategy.** An additional benefit of standardization is that customers see a consistent marketing strategy. Use of a global brand, global identity, and global product features may add value as customers travel across

international borders. Exposure to the same messages strengthens brand identity. Conversely, inconsistency in marketing strategies might create dissatisfaction. If customers in different markets realize they are paying different prices, they may feel the offering to them is over-priced. Such differences in prices may also cause them to question the value of the brand itself.

Gray markets and Umbro football shirts

Gray markets are perfectly legal although a potential irritant to marketers who craft pricing strategies based on differences in the ability or willingness of customers in different markets to pay for a particular product or service. The term refers to "arbitrage," where agents, wholesales, retailers, or other traders buy goods legally at a cheaper price in one market, and supply them into another international market where that good is sold by the marketer at a higher price, or is unavailable.

In the run up to the 2006 FIFA World Cup, Umbro, manufacturers of the England football shirt, launched a new red England away shirt. The new shirt was selling via the Football Association for around £30 in England. English retailer Asda, however, used the gray market to buy up shirts from Europe and sell them again in the United Kingdom, also doing so before the official launch of the shirt in the United Kingdom. This situation can arise either through a price differential, or as seems likely here, where the manufacturer makes extra shirts and sells these to other companies that have no link with the official channel (http://www.bized.co.uk/dataserv/chron/news/2546.htm, http://news.bbc.co.uk/1/low/business/4789878.stm).

- **Better technology and better traveled customers.** As customers can travel anywhere in the world within a day, and follow any company or sport via the Internet regardless of their time zone or geographic distance from the home of the team, customers will seek out the brands they value, and the market will determine which brands they find attractive.
- **Improved planning and control.** Buzzell cites the example of Philips Lighting, which at one stage in its history found its

German subsidiary undercutting prices charged by the Dutch subsidiary by 30 percent. At the very least the company may cannibalize sales in one market by actions in another, but it may also result in needless duplication of advertising and marketing materials, websites and other marketing tools.

- **Exploiting good ideas.** If there is a premium on innovative ideas or successful products and services, then those that work should be exploited to maximum effect. Buzzell argues against the use of average ideas if the firm has better ideas globally.

Conversely, global marketers have argued *against* standardization of the marketing offer on these bases:

- **A lack of evidence of homogenization** (Douglas and Wind 1987). While some argue about the existence of global consumers with similar needs and wants, contradictory evidence suggests a trend towards greater fragmentation of markets. Customers increasingly wish to be individual, and might rebel against the idea of universal global brands in favor of local and more individualistic affiliation.
- **Market characteristics.** Even if arguments based on customer convergence are accepted, some national differences persist. Some characteristics such as geographic distance, level of technology, restrictive government, and level of economic development may impact on the ability of individual customers to engage with a particular brand.
- **Value of economies of scale?** While global standardization may offer some cost benefits, marketers have also argued against the extent of the economies of scale that can be gained. As websites still need cultural and linguistic adaptation, and media space is still a major component of advertising cost, regardless of whether a standardized brand or message is used, the savings may make it ineffective to standardize purely on the basis of cost benefit.

Are there global sports?

This may sound like a strange question. Surely the Football World Cup, the Olympics, the games of football (soccer), basketball, and others must be global? This depends, however, on the definition of global used by researchers.

By some definitions, global refers only to the number of countries in which a company operates, or perhaps to the geographic areas in which it is available. Kenichi Ohmae (1985) argues that to be global a firm must operate in all parts of the Triad, that is in North America, Europe, and Japan, although others have extended this to include East Asia more broadly.

Global may, however, be used to refer to the way in which a firm has divided up its areas of activity between different geographic regions, with perhaps research and development in one country, sales and distribution on a local basis, and marketing coordinated regionally or globally (Rugman 1986). It is this last definition that has led some researchers to argue that a majority of sports are regional, not global. Indeed Rugman argues that football, or soccer, is not global because the game is played and positioned differently in the United States (where it is mainly viewed as a woman's sport and participation sport) whereas the man's game is higher profile and has a large number of spectators as well as players in most other countries.

Despite such arguments, there can be few doubts that sport is increasingly global. Westerbeck and Smith (2003: 6) point out:

> Over the last decades sport has probably been the element of culture that has progressed further, fastest. Spurred on by ego, individual and national, sport has crossed virtually every border. Disseminated through radio and television, sport has become universal.

They point to trends, such as increasing discretionary spend and leisure time, improved infrastructure, especially in wealthier nations, and global media that make accessible a wide range of sports. Despite the current global recession, many of these trends continue. Indeed the commercial development of football has continued as we go into 2010, and while there are some indications of harder times ahead with the demise of Setanta Sports and increased job losses, it is yet to be seen whether the current economic downturn will significantly affect football finances.

As in many other sectors, technological advances have played a major role in creating global audiences for sports. Later in this chapter, the development of virtual communities is discussed. Even if fans live too far away from their favorite club to attend matches, they can still share their passion with like-minded fans via the Internet. These global communities provide an ideal means of finding out about, watching, and discussing football brands regardless of where the fan is based.

Forbes Magazine's evaluation of the most successful sports brands makes interesting reading. The recent 2007 ranking shows a range of successful sports brands. In sports teams, for example, ESPN tops the rankings, followed by Nike, Adidas, Inder Armour, and EA Sports.

Among the sports events, these are spread across sports, with many of the major global tournaments topping the ranks as discussed below.

To arrive at these figures, Forbes used methods of quantitative analysis similar to those used to assess the value of brands in other sectors. Brand values measure the equity built up in a name over years, or decades. Forbes comments that it values sports events on the basis of the revenue they generate per event day. On this basis, despite the length of the Summer Olympics and the World Cup tournament, the Super Bowl generates more revenue pro rata than the Olympics or Football World Cup. This revenue comes from broadcasting and online rights, sponsorship, and merchandising, as well as gate receipts.

Individual stars' brand values are based on the amount by which the endorsement income of the sports' star in the past year has exceeded the average level for their peers.

On this basis (according to *Forbes Magazine*, September 29, 2007, "The world's top sports brands"), the highest ranked global sports events are:

1. The Super Bowl (with a value of US$336 million).
2. The Summer Olympics (value US$176 million).
3. The FIFA World Cup (value US£103 million).

Among the individual sports stars, although footballers David Beckham ($18 million) and Ronaldinho ($9 million) make the top ten, their earnings are dwarfed by those of top-ranked Tiger

Woods ($164 million), and Phil Mickelson (golf), Roger Federer (tennis), LeBron James (basketball), and Maria Sharapova (tennis) divide the two football stars in the ranking.

On a similar basis, *Forbes* calculated the value of sports teams. To do this, it took out any revenue that was not directly linked to the team's brand name – such as revenue shared jointly with others in the league (as is the case for US sports including Major League Soccer). On this basis, the most successful global sports teams in the world are:

1. Manchester United FC in England (with an estimated brand value of US$351 million).
2. Real Madrid, of Spain (estimated brand value of US$288 million).
3. Bayern Munich of Germany (estimated brand value of US$217 million).
4. New York Yankees American Football team (estimated brand value of US$217 million).
5. Arsenal Football Club (estimated brand value US$185 million).

While these are not the most up-to-date figures, the *Forbes* (2007) data are interesting as a comparison of the relative global size of football brands and the brands of other global sports teams. Football, and specifically European football brands, dominate the team rankings much more than in the rankings of individual stars or sporting events. No fewer than six of the ten teams are from European football, with the top three all being football brands. Only the New York Yankees (American football), Dallas Cowboys (American football), Boston Red Sox (baseball), and Washington Redskins (American football) make the top ten sports brands.

A more transparent understanding of the figures relating to the largest football brands can be gained from the Deloitte and Touche's Football Money League 2009.

Deloitte (200) notes that the revenues of the English clubs in Table 5.1 are depressed by the poor pound sterling to euro exchange rate when this was calculated compared with the previous year. Without this, Manchester United

Table 5.1 Top European football clubs by revenue

Rank 2007–08	Club	Revenue (million)
1	Real Madrid	365.8
2	Manchester United	324.8
3	FC Barcelona	308.8
4	Bayern Munich	295.3
5	Chelsea	268.9
6	Arsenal	264.4
7	Liverpool	210.9
8	AC Milan	209.5
9	AS Roma	175.4
10	Internazionale	172.9

Source: Based on data drawn from Deloitte and Touche's Money League 2009.

would be much closer to, or even above, Real Madrid in Table 5.1.

We can conclude that sport is global but there remain challenges for its development as a market. For example, the market research NPD group in 2009 commented that women have a relatively restricted time in which to develop a sporting interest as a larger number of women – particularly in some markets – might juggle the home and childcare alongside work.

Such cultural, societal, and historical issues play a role in many sports. For example, some sports have particular origins and associations with countries or regions. Despite several attempts to grow football (soccer) in the United States, the sport remains different in nature and less dominant than in Europe, Latin America, or East Asia. It may, however, be gaining in popularity in the United States relative to sports such as hockey. Sports have strong cultural identity and roots, and many sports are of interest only in cultural subgroupings, such as rugby and cricket in current or former Commonwealth nations, and baseball and basketball predominantly in North America. Other sports are specific to particular regions or countries, such as rodeo, Sumo wrestling, and Australian Rules football, and remain as niche interests.

Sport has certainly been used as a tool for globalization by many companies as they seek to expand. They are attracted by the popularity of sport and the way in which is makes a direct association with people's attitudes (Bainbridge 1997).

Globalization of football

Do the above trends in globalization of sport suggest that football is indeed a global game with global brands?

Football is the world's most popular sport. Since the late 19th century the game has expanded across the globe. Several countries, including England, China, and Argentina, claim early forms of the game that they have been responsible for diffusing around the world. Whoever popularized the game first, it is clear that football is now a "global game" which spans culturally diverse societies in all continents. FIFA refers to an estimated 250 million participating in the game, and around 1.4 billion people worldwide who have an interest in football globally. The financial and cultural significance of the game is huge – the FIFA World Cup was watched on television in 166 countries in 1986, but in 214 by 2006. The television audience almost doubled from 13.5 billion to 26.288 billion (although interestingly these figures reached a height of 28.843 billion for the 2002 World Cup (http://www.fifa.com/mm/document/fifafacts/ffprojects/ip-401_05a_tvstats_9299.pdf).

Alongside the economic ramifications of broadcast and sponsorship that go with these figures, culturally, it is easy to find evidence of the global influence of football. During the 2002 World Cup in Japan and South Korea, David Beckham's Mohawk hairstyle was instantly taken up by Japanese adolescents. Foer (2004) even cites the appearance of Beckham statuettes in Buddhist temples in Bangkok, Thailand. The image and appeal of individual players, or team brands, can appeal across a diverse range of cultures. Indeed, Giulianotti and Robertson (2004) argue that football plays an important role in globalization and should be discussed alongside music, fashion, travel, technology, and other forces that have helped to create the "global village" (Ohmae 1985) in which we live.

Alongside the consumer, demand-side, the governance, competition, and supply-side factors in football are also global.

The governance of the game of football has been organized on a regional and global basis since the late 1940s, when clubs began to compete against each other in frequent regional competitions through UEFA (the Union of European Football) and its Latin American, African, and Asian counterparts. FIFA's (the Fédération Internationale de Football Association's) World Cup continues strongly, with intense competition between countries and regions to host future tournaments.

Globalization has also grown in the supply side of football. Top global teams are no longer made up of players from the local area, or even the nation, but contain individuals identified by sophisticated global scouting systems. This phenomenon is not new. Nor is the concern that global football teams might affect the development of national football. The Spanish dictator Franco banned imports of foreign players into Spain in the 1950s, the Brazilian government legally prohibited Pelé from being sold in the early 1960s, and recently Andy Burnham (until June 2009, the English culture and sport secretary) posed a set of questions to the Premier League and Football League which included discussion of whether a certain quota of English players should be included in each club in order to safeguard the future development of young English football players.

Indeed the debate whether the market for football players should be a free market globally, or subject to labor restrictions, is long-standing. Sepp Blatter, the president of FIFA, is an advocate of a six plus five system which would see all European clubs fielding six native players in each game, whilst others argue that, while homegrown talent should be encouraged, this would be an artificial intervention if these players would not have gained their places in the team on merit. The first English league team to comprise entirely non-English players was Accrington Stanley in 1955 – the team were all-Scottish, as was the manager (*Guardian,* May 18, 2009). The first club to field a non-English team in recent times was Chelsea, on Boxing Day 1999, when Gianluca Vialli selected a team that did not include any English players. In May 2009, Manchester United fielded a non-English team in the Manchester derby match, for the first time in their history. This trend can also be seen in Italian and Spanish football. Indeed it is entirely to be expected that the most successful football leagues in the world attract the best players in the world,

In the current era, capital in the football market flows across national borders in a way similar to that described by Ohmae (1985). Indeed this goes beyond Ohmae's Triad (North America, Europe, and Japan, which he argued formed 80 percent of the world's trade flows) to comprise growing trade between the Triad and other nations from East Asia, Africa, Latin America, and the rest of the world. There is increasing interest in the development of emerging nations such as China, and, to a lesser extent given its lesser historical interest in football, India.

The focus on emerging markets such as China parallels the broader interest in these mega markets. In football terms, China is currently center stage, given its size and its tradition of football support. India tends to be associated with support for cricket and hockey, although it should be noted that there is an increasing interest in football among younger supporters, particularly centered on viewing in bars and the formation of grassroots academies.

Glocalization

While football has globalized and there is evidence of strong global football brands, there is no suggestion that fans have become homogenous across the globe. When Levitt (1983) argued that customers across the globe have become the same as each other because they wear similar fashions, listen to similar music, and can travel anywhere in the world within a day, critics pointed to opposing evidence which suggests that customers see themselves as increasingly individual and have fragmented in their tastes.

Similarly in the football market, while global brands such as Real Madrid, AC Milan, and Argentina may appeal to fans across the globe, some fans may be as fervent in their support of football, but of their local team. Yet others may tread a middle path, supporting an internationally renowned team, but taking a local interest in it. So, for example, South Korean fans may support Manchester United but have a particular interest in Ji-Sung Park.

There is a now an increasing awareness that some of the

assumptions of previous studies of "football fandom" may be shifting as the globalization of the game continues apace. This bias in popular discussions and research into the nature of fandom is highlighted among others by Williams (2007) and Giulianotti (2002).

It is easy for locally based fans to assume that they are in some way "better" or "more loyal" supporters of a team, than those fans who live in places geographically distant from the club. This could be on the basis of regular match attendance. Yet sometimes, fans would acknowledge the merits of a particular fan who used to live locally but now lives a hemisphere away for work or other reasons. Such a person has proven their "true fan" credentials and may have family or cultural affinity to the area. What, however, if the person has never been to the country, let alone the town or city, where the club is based? The following sections consider this "dislocated" support, where fans support football clubs in other countries and regions, and also the mid-ground between global brands and local clubs.

As with other areas of international marketing, the key challenge is to balance the global/universal with the local and particular. This challenge is often referred to as "glocalization," a mid-path between total standardization and local adaptation of the marketing offer. Glocalization was proposed as the optimum solution by authors including Quelch and Hoff (1986), Douglas and Wind (1987), Ohmae (1985), and Riesenbeck and Freeling (1991). This choice would afford savings where possible, without going to the extremes proposed by Levitt (1983) and losing the flexibility to appeal to culturally different customers in different markets.

Quelch and Hoff (1986) suggest that the extent of standardization of products and services depends on both their nature and the cultural similarity of the markets. Industrial products and commodities are the easiest to standardize globally. Products and services consumed in the home, such as food, are more culturally sensitive. Whilst questioning the applicability of global standardization, Douglas and Wind (1987) accept that it may be more possible to find global segments in "high-technology" and "high-touch," or luxury, niches. Yip (1989) suggests that the extent to which a firm's customers, channels, and competitors are global may dictate the extent to which consistency is desirable and necessary. On this basis, many aspects of football fit with the "high-touch" niche status products, where the glamorous lifestyles of players and their celebrity wives and girlfriends make them aspirational figures for fans, and the universal appeal of the game speaks to fans regardless of their language and culture.

International football tournaments demonstrate a particular balance between the local and universal. For example, Giulianotti and Robertson (2004) argue that:

> However polyethnic a single society may be, its individual members are each expected to identify with a specific national team. At major international tournaments, thousands of different supporter groups co-mingle, with each nation displaying distinctive kinds of dress, song, music and patterns of behavior (such as in their relations with local people, other supporter groups, and the various security forces).

The authors argue that "glocal" behavior can be seen when we all discuss the same global football tournament, but do so with a particular focus on players who are our local heroes or hopes for the competition.

Perhaps related to this is the idea that this "belonging" to a group may not be linked to a particular nationality identity. (See Chapter 3 for a fuller discussion on modern tribes.) Among Chinese fans, for example, the concept of a "second team" is commonplace. Fans of local Chinese teams and the Chinese national football team might support a different national team in a tournament in which their own team is not playing. In the 2002 World Cup, it was not unusual to see groups of young Japanese and South Korean fans in the adopted colors of their favored team, be that Italy, Holland, or Argentina. The following case study looks at some of the fan support behavior shown by Chinese fans at the time of the 2006 World Cup in Germany. The Chinese national team did not play in this competition, and football fans in the country then had to decide whether to support a different team or none at all during this competition. If so, was this a team that they followed only for this competition. or a "second team" with which they identified more broadly, and on what basis do fans decide which team to support?

The "second team" pattern of support seen among Asian fans seems to be different from the rivalry between, say, English and Scottish fans, whereby when Scotland did not qualify for a particular World Cup, some Scottish fans chose to support any team who were playing against England rather than choosing a different national team to follow throughout the tournament.

Chinese fans of international football

This case study explores general awareness levels for international teams in China. It should be remembered that this research was conducted during the 2006 World Cup, which may have increased awareness of international football teams compared with periods when international teams attract less media coverage.

Awareness was tested using a range of different techniques. These included prompted and unprompted recall as well as different types of constrained choice (team seen most, top three teams, recall as many teams as you can), and measures of frequency with which teams are seen in China.

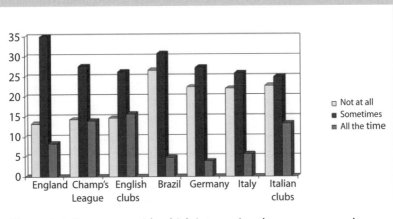

Figure 5.1 Frequency with which international teams are seen in China

Table 5.2 Top 20 international football teams seen most frequently on television or in the news in China

Rank order	Team	Percentage of respondents
1	England	27.2
3	Italy	11.2
4	Manchester United	9.5
5	Germany	5.1
6	AC Milan	4.1
7	Other	3.7
8	Real Madrid	3.7
9	Argentina	3.1
10	Chelsea	2.7
11	Spain	2.7
12	Inter Milan	2.4
13	Juventus	2.0
13	France	2.0
13	Arsenal	2.0
13	South Korea	2.0
13	Barcelona	2.0
18	Liverpool	1.4
19	Holland	1.0
20	Japan	0.7

None of the international football formats is seen in China all the time or even most of the time. The highest scores for teams that were seen "all the time" were for English club football (15.73 percent of respondents) and Champions League (13.99 percent). International teams had higher awareness during major tournaments, but then the highest score was still only 16.43 percent (Italy) and 16.08 percent for the England national team, followed by Germany, Argentina, and Brazil in that order.

The highest responses were for people who were aware of seeing coverage of both national and club sides "sometimes" in China. For sides seen "sometimes" England had the highest score (almost 35 percent of respondents saw coverage of England sometimes), followed by Brazil (almost 31 percent), and then Champions League (27.62 percent), Germany (27.27 percent), and English club football (26.22 percent).

Respondents were asked to list the three teams that they were most aware of in China. As this was unprompted it included mentions of many different types of teams, including Chinese local and national teams, international clubs, and national

Table 5.3 How frequently do you see coverage of these international teams?

Team	Not at all %	Not often %	Sometimes %	Most of the time %	During major tournaments %	All the time %
England national team	13.27	17.13	34.97	10.14	16.08	8.39
Champions League	14.34	14.69	27.62	17.83	9.40	13.99
English club football	14.69	14.69	26.22	18.53	9.09	15.73
Brazilian national team	26.57	16.78	30.7	5.94	11.50	4.80
Brazilian club football	43.36	31.81	14.34	3.50	2.10	1.05
Spanish national team	26.92	23.43	22.73	7.69	11.19	2.45
Spanish club football	27.27	17.13	20.98	14.34	7.69	8.39
Argentinian national team	31.82	20.28	22.38	4.89	11.88	3.85
Argentinian club football	46.15	28.32	13.63	4.89	2.45	0.35
Italian national team	22.02	17.13	25.87	9.79	16.43	5.59
Italian club football	22.72	12.59	24.83	13.98	9.79	13.29
German national team	22.38	19.93	27.27	8.39	13.99	3.84
German club football	24.83	21.68	20.28	9.79	11.19	7.69

teams. Among the Chinese clubs identified were Shanghai Shenhua, Shandong Luneng, Dalian Shide, and Beijing Guoan, although these were mentioned only once or twice each. In this case study, we focus on the international sides that were identified, and the percentage of respondents who listed these among the teams that they see on television or in the news in China (see Table 5.2). The unprompted ranking places England highest with 27.2 percent, followed by Italy (11.2 percent), and then Manchester United (9.5 percent)

Levels of interest in sport

The levels of interest in sport indicated by the respondents are shown in Table 5.4. Around 78 percent of respondents have some level of interest in international football (that is they score themselves as quite, very, or extremely interested), compared with 31.24 percent who are interested in watching local football.

Table 5.4 Respondents' level of interest in sport and football

	Not at all interested %	Not very interested %	Quite interested %	Very interested %	Extremely interested %
Sport	1.15	12.68	40.06	29.11	17.00
Playing sport	3.33	15.76	35.45	31.21	14.24
Football	6.02	24.10	24.70	21.69	23.49
Playing football	24.58	28.24	19.93	13.95	13.29
Watching local football	31.53	37.24	16.22	8.41	6.61
Watching international football	3.92	18.07	24.40	30.12	23.49

Level of interest in and involvement with Chinese local football

Data are analyzed in two ways. First, data are analyzed to identify the total frequency of involvement in different activities relating to Chinese local football (see Table 5.5). Respondents were requested to tick all of those in which they engaged (so the total frequency scores are higher than the total number of observations). The activities of each individual were then analyzed to identify a level of "engagement" with Chinese local football (Table 5.6). Just over a third of respondents were not interested in Chinese local football, compared with 15.9 percent who were heavily involved in it – although only a small proportion actually attended matches – and a majority (just over 40 percent) who engaged in one or more activities such as reading about Chinese local football in newspapers or watching matches on television, but did not attend matches.

Table 5.5 Activities relating to Chinese local football

Activity	Frequency
Attending matches	21
Watching on television	135
Watching on the Internet	41
Listen to it on the radio	22
Read about it in the newspapers	123
I am interested but do none of these	23
I am not interested	114
Total	479

Table 5.6 Level of engagement with Chinese local football

Activity	Percentage of respondents
Attend matches and other activity	15.9
Engage in four activities	1.16
Engage in three activitities	2.3
Engage in two activities	16.76
Engage in one activity	23.6
Interested but not active	4.9
I am not interested	35.26

Support for the Chinese national football team

A higher number of respondents indicated support for the Chinese national football team compared with local Chinese football (70.64 percent compared with 31.24 percent) (see Table 5.7).

Activity levels involving the Chinese national team were, however, less frequent than for Chinese local football. Table 5.8 shows the total frequency reported for the different activities relating to the Chinese national football team.

Table 5.7 Level of support for the Chinese national football team

Do you follow the Chinese football team?	Percentage of respondents
Yes	70.64
No	29.32

Table 5.8 Activities relating to Chinese national football team

Activity	Frequency %
Attending matches	4
Watching on television	51
Watching on the Internet	7
Listen to it on the radio	1
Read about it in the newspapers	25
I am interested but do none of these	5
Total	93

Although there were only 93 reports of support activity relating to Chinese national football (see Table 5.8) compared with 365 reports for Chinese local football (see Table 5.5 – a total of 479 less the 114 who said that they were not interested) , this relatively low level of activity in relation to the Chinese national team may be because of the tournaments are less frequent and matches more distant than those for local football.

As can be seen in Table 5.9, only a small proportion of

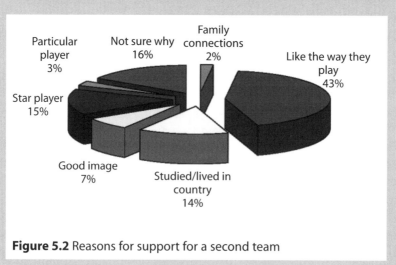

Figure 5.2 Reasons for support for a second team

Table 5.9 Support for other international teams at major
            tournaments

Rank order	Team	Percentage of respondents
1	England	26.35
2	Brazil	20.61
3	Argentina	11.82
4	Germany	10.81
4	Italy	10.81
6	France	6.41
7	Holland	3.04
8	Spain	2.03
8	Portugal	2.03
10	Other	1.01
11	South Korea	0.68
12	Japan	0
	If China are not playing, I do not support a team	3.7

Table 5.10 Reasons for support of a second international team

Reasons for support	Percentage
I have family connections there	1.98
I like the way they play	39.6
I studied or lived there	12.54
They have a good image	6.27
They have star players	13.2
My friends support this team	2.64
I like a particular player	9.24
Not sure why, I just like them	14.52

respondents (3.7 percent) did not support a team in major tournaments when China was not playing. The most popular "second team" to support in tournaments such as World Cup 2006 was England (26.35 percent), followed by Brazil (20.61 percent), Argentina, Italy, and Germany. Respondents were also asked to explain, if they could, the reason for the choice of second team they supported (see Table 5.10).

The dominant reason for support was that a respondent liked the way a team played (39.6 percent). The second largest response was that the respondent could not give any particular reason for their support (14.52 percent "Not sure why, I just like them"). Star players accounted for 13.2 percent of respondents, with having studied and lived in a country, and liking particular players, also being given as reasons for supporting a particular team.

Global football brands in China

When asked about the international sides that they supported, many Chinese fans also talked about international club sides they supported or whose shirts they commonly saw in the country. None of the shirts were seen "all the time," but a number of international football brands were seen "very often" in the Chinese market, as fans wear the shirts of these teams. The most commonly seen shirts were England, Brazil, Manchester United, and Italy, then AC Milan and Real Madrid (see Table 5.11).

Table 5.11 Whose shirts do you commonly see in China?

Team	Not at all %	Not often %	Often %	Very often %	All the time %
China	24.48	46.85	16.43	9.79	2.10
Argentina	13.29	29.37	35.66	17.13	2.09
Inter Milan	13.29	32.17	30.07	17.13	2.79
England	5.94	11.19	32.87	40.56	8.74
Real Madrid	13.29	19.93	29.72	25.17	7.3
Italy	10.14	18.18	36.04	29.72	4.19
Chelsea	21.00	36.71	18.18	15.38	3.15
Brazil	8.39	17.83	32.52	30.42	9.79
Manchester Utd	9.09	18.53	28.67	30.42	11.19
Barcelona	16.43	30.77	27.62	16.78	4.54
Spain	18.18	43.71	23.08	10.14	1.05
AC Milan	10.84	23.08	29.72	25.52	6.99
Germany	13.97	33.92	31.47	16.08	2.1
France	15.04	34.96	30.07	16.43	1.75
Other	24.28	28.67	15.73	4.9	2.1

Other club sides listed included Barcelona, Inter Milan, Chelsea, Arsenal, and Liverpool. When asked to identify "other" clubs whose shirts they saw people wearing in China, the list included Juventus, Barcelona, Bayern Munich, Werder Bremen, Borussia Dortmund, Hertha Berlin, Croatia, Ajax, and Fiorentina. (Source: Bridgewater 2004.)

Among other evidence of the "glocalization" of football, Giulianotti and Robertson (2004) refer to the increasing role of transnational corporations in football. So, for example, Nike, Adidas, and Umbro are major players in terms of football merchandise. BSkyB, which is part-owned by Rupert Murdoch's News International Ltd, and even larger clubs may have global brands. From 2000 to 2008 the world's largest football clubs were represented by a legally established body, the G-14, based in Brussels. The G-14 was created in 2000 by the three clubs from Italy's top division along with two each from France, Germany, Spain, Holland, and England, and one from Portugal. The purpose of the organization was to provide a unified voice in negotiations with UEFA and FIFA. New members were only admitted by invitation, and in 2002 four more clubs were invited to join to make 18 members, although the original G-14 name was retained. The membership of G-14 included original members Liverpool, Manchester United, Juventus, AC Milan and Internazionale, Marseille, Paris St Germain, Bayern Munich, Borussia Dortmund, Ajax, PSV Eindhoven, Barcelona, Real Madrid, and Porto, and the later entrants from 2002, Arsenal, Lyon, Bayer Leverkusen, and Valencia. The G-14 disbanded on February 15, 2008, and was replaced by the European Club Association. This represents 103 clubs from all 53 UEFA nations.

These transnational corporations have evolved their own distinctive ways of marketing across borders, and are the hub of global communities of fans. In terms of ownership, a new trend has emerged whereby the largest clubs are owned by international investors, and these investors often own portfolios of sports brands (although football laws currently prohibit them from owning multiple football brands). These new global sports corporations may create new alliances between different sports and different regions, thereby changing the context of global football marketing.

Manchester United

Manchester United (MU) is one of the most popular and well-known global football brands. It has unrivalled levels of recognition and support among fans around the world, and is clearly the number one brand in the number one game in the world.

The club's vision and values are that it should be "the best football club in the world both on and off the pitch," and in achieving its aims, Manchester United not only compares itself with other football clubs, but also aims to innovate and establish best practice in relation to brand leaders in other popular sports, such as Formula One, American football, basketball, and baseball, to look at best practice and innovation of the brand. Football, as a game, is the world's leading sport in that its followers span all parts of the globe, whereas some of the major US sports have a main concentration of fans within the North American region.

The club encapsulates its vision and values in the following acronym:

United…	with our fans in our commitment and passion for the club
Non-discriminatory…	in making Manchester United accessible to all, irrespective of age, race, gender, creed or physical ability
Innovative…	in our ambition to be "first to the ball" at all times
Team-oriented…	in our desire to work together with the same dedication displayed in every game by our first team squad
Excelling…	in our aim to be world-class in everything we do
Determined…	in our pursuit of success while being accountable for our actions

Building brand relationships

Such is the success of the MU brand that its impact extends far beyond football. The brand values of the club transcend sport, and the club works with major multinational corporations in a range of sectors. It should be noted that commentators looking at the strength of Manchester United's brand tend to over-estimate the size of the club itself, comparing it with Coca-Cola or Wal-Mart. In fact, Manchester United, football's brand leader, is closer in size to a small or medium-sized enterprise (it has 550 employees and an annual turnover of around £300 million compared with Wal-Mart's $351.1 billion turnover, larger than the gross national income (GNI) of Austria and more than twice the size of the GNI in Argentina or New Zealand).

The strength of the MU brand has created opportunities for fruitful business relationships with much larger organizations in other sectors. Until the end of the 2009–10 season, the club's sponsor was AIG which, until the global economic downturn, was the fourth largest US firm by market capitalization. Despite AIG's size, it was not well known as a brand and benefited from the cooperation by gaining much greater awareness of its brand. Vodafone, the previous sponsor of Manchester United, was a leading UK phone company and was supported in its global acquisition strategy by the values and positive associations that Manchester United has in its target markets. In establishing this type of brand association, Manchester United considers why the prospective partner wishes to work with the club.

The rationale for building relationships frequently extends beyond simply building brand awareness for the partner into more strategic aims, such as mutual reinforcement of brand values. For example, the collaboration between Manchester United and Diageo's Smirnoff vodka in Asia focused on a respon-sible drinking campaign, and used the sporting profession-alism of Manchester United's players to reinforce the message that drinking excessively is dangerous and in no one's best interests.

Below the level of its main sponsor relationship, Manchester United has a range of brand relationships, some global and others that work on a regional or country basis. Manchester United has established a relationship with Saudi Telecom which encompasses a standard sponsorship agreement plus the development of unique, MU-specific content to be offered to subscribers in Saudi Arabia – a country where there are substantial numbers of MU fans. This idea has already been rolled out in India, Indonesia, and Nigeria and will doubtless extend to other territories over time. Another such regional relationship was that between Manchester United and Audi UK. While this was initially funded out of the United Kingdom and involved some players driving Audi cars, the relationship worked so well that it has now been rolled out across the Audi group worldwide. Audi has also had a longstanding relationship in Germany with Bayern Munich and other leading European clubs, and held the inaugural Audi Cup in Germany in July 2009 to celebrate its centenary.

Brand development since 1992

The strength of the MU brand owes a great deal to the long and illustrious history of the football club and to the emotional value that the brand gains from the memories and associations that fans have with great teams, great players, and managers. The Busby Babes, Sir Bobby Charlton, Sir Alex Ferguson, and generations of league and cup-winning teams combine to create a unique heritage for Manchester United.

Since 1992, the development of the Premier League has also contributed to the development of the MU brand. Formed in 1992, the top English League, the Premier League, has grown to be the world's most successful football league. In 2007–08 the revenue of the Premier League increased by 26 per cent to £1,932 million. The most recent Deloitte and Touche Football Finance Report (2009) shows a combined revenue for the "big five" football leagues (Italy's Serie A, Spain's La Liga, Germany's Bundesliga, and France's Ligue 1) of €7.7 billion in 2007/08.

The success of all of these leagues continues apace – with a 10 percent year on year growth in revenue from 2006/07 – the largest absolute increase since 1999/2000.

The position of the Premier League as the "highest revenue generating league in the world" (Deloitte and Touche 2009) was strengthened in 2007/08 as it extended the gap between itself and the next three leagues to more than €1 billion.

To play in a well-managed and successful league, such as

the Premier League, confers benefits on the clubs within the league. There is a flow of money to the clubs within the league from broadcasting deals. Each of the clubs within the league benefits from the collective broadcasting deals that are set up by the league (these are pro rata according to finishing league position, from around £50 million for the top league position to around £30 million for the 20th placed club). In some countries, such as Spain, individual clubs do their own broadcasting deals, and more successful teams might be expected to gain substantially compared with lower placed teams. This does not, however, favor the overall health and competitive balance of the league. As around one quarter of the Premier League's £1 billion revenue comes from overseas markets, there would still seem to be potential for the Premier League to become even more commercially successful, to the benefit of the clubs within the league.

A focus on football

Within Manchester United, being a football club is at the heart of everything the club does. Commercial development of the brand allows the club to bring football and involvement with Manchester United to a broader set of fans, but this must sit alongside the traditional behaviors and footballing values of the club. Accordingly, on the pitch, the club is committed to ensuring that the team is equipped to compete for major trophies each year, that it can attract the most talented and innovative manager and coaching staff, alongside maintaining a playing squad of the highest caliber by attracting young and established players from around the world, and by developing the best talent through the club's youth academy.

To this end, the recent successful four-year period in the club's development has seen reinvestment back into the stadium as well as in players and player contracts which help the club to achieve its sporting aims. If the club considers the option of playing friendly football matches in other countries, such as overseas tours, they are driven in destination and character by Sir Alex Ferguson and his coaching staff. But the club also uses tours to provide added value to its commercial partners, as well as providing a platform for its charitable foundation to help far-flung communities with an affinity to the club tackle real social problems that they face.

Social responsibility

Manchester United has three pillars – the company, the community, and its work in the charity sector. The charitable side of the club's work is now organized through the MU Foundation. Formed to celebrate the 50th anniversary of the club being the first English side to play in European competitions, the MU Foundation aims to use the passion for Manchester United to educate, motivate, and inspire young people to build a better life for themselves and improve the communities they live in. The Foundation delivers football coaching, skills training, personal development, and life-changing experiences, providing young people with opportunities to change their lives for the better. Through football, the Foundation encourages young people to develop as players and more importantly as people. The goal of the Foundation is to educate, motivate and inspire future generations to build better communities for all.

In its charitable activities, Manchester United has relationships at global, national, and local levels. Internationally, the club has a ten-year relationship with UNICEF, which uses players to help it to fundraise and to promote its aims to improve the health, education, and position of children in difficulty across the world. This relationship is estimated to have impacted positively on the lives of over 1.5 million children around the world, in countries including China, India, Thailand, Laos, Vietnam, South Africa, Mozambique, and Afghanistan. Projects on which Manchester United has worked with UNICEF include work with children affected by disasters such as the 2004 tsunami, children living in poverty, and those at risk of exploitation or without access to education. Since 2005, the club has supported UNICEF's global campaign "Unite for Children, Unite against Aids." In addition to the club's support for UNICEF, Sir Alex Ferguson, Ryan Giggs, Dimitar Berbatov, and Ole Gunnar Solskjaer are ambassadors for the charity.

Alongside this global cooperation, the club also has

successful charitable relationships at a national level with the Children's Society and the Cystic Fibrosis Trust, while it also has more locally based charitable relationships, with the Christie Hospital in Manchester – one of Europe's leading cancer centers –with the appeal for funds to build a new children's hospital in Manchester, with Francis House, and to support Rainbow House, a charity with centers in the North-West of England, in Chorley, Cumbria, and Clitheroe, which helps children with neurological disorders with learning.

The future

Despite the wide array of relationships and activities in which the club currently participates, CEO David Gill still sees that there are "so many things left that we can work on and so many ways in which we can continue to develop the Manchester United brand, without ever losing sight of the fact that we are, fundamentally, a football club."

Some of the areas for future development relate to techno-logical advances. While the Club's commitment to the collective selling of the television rights to Football Association Premier League (FAPL) matches is sacrosanct, as technology converges, so more of the non-TV media rights revert back to clubs and might be used to develop new areas of activity for the club and its commercial partners. The global success of the MU brand means that there are always new markets opening up in which the club can establish mutually beneficial relationships with partner organizations, on a local, regional, or potentially global basis. Moreover, the club never loses sight of the importance of creating excellent match-day experiences for its fans, and continually improves the comfort and safety of Old Trafford's stadium facilities.

Off the pitch, Manchester United's vision is to create a busi-ness culture that satisfies the needs of all of its stakeholders – including fans, its owners, the wider football family, and staff – to increase the understanding of the needs and grow the size of its fanbase around the world, and to be an active member of the broader community. The vision for the future of Manchester United involves combining the core values of the club, which have helped it to develop into such a successful and professionally run club, with the outlook it needs to give its fans and wider customer base the excellent experience they deserve. This vision has football at its very heart: "We aim to be the best football club in the world both on and off the pitch."

Global fans

One of the key recent debates in football concerns fans of clubs who are based in other countries, and who may never have attended a match or even been to the country of origin of their preferred team.

While some would argue that these fans cannot be as loyal as traditional supporters, they often show similar patterns of support. One Australian colleague, in discussing his support of Arsenal, explained that his father was also an Arsenal supporter – and had come from London – and that his support was, therefore, the same father–son type of support often seen in clubs, albeit that the generations had moved geographically. Another Cypriot Manchester United fan emphasized that, while he had never lived in England or had family connections with Manchester, he was the third generation of his family to support the club, he attended regular supporters club events in Cyprus, some attended by Sir Alex Ferguson, watched all televised matches via satellite television, and considered himself to have a strong behavioral and emotional tie to the club.

Logically, these global fans may be just as fervently attached to clubs. Indeed the way in which all fans demonstrate their support may be different now, in reflection of different times and technology, than that shown in our grandparents' times. So why do some see these fans as "less loyal" or "less true" than themselves?

Maybe this is simply a part of the internalizing of success (Cialdini et al. 1976) in which all fans indulge – "I am clearly very important to the success of the team" – and all fans believe that they are more loyal than the person who sits next to them at a match on some basis or other – attending more matches, traveling more miles, spending more money, suffering more, feeling the pain or joy of support more intensely than the next person.

Fans who cannot physically attend matches often use technology to find out about and share in the activities of their club. Giulianotti (2002) refers to this type of fan as "flâneurs" (strollers), taking in football experiences, often through the virtual arena. While these virtual fans clearly exist – I refer to them in Chapter 2 as e-loyal fans, and many e-loyal fans are so because they are based in other countries – it is not, however, clear that virtual support means detached or less than "real" support or emotional attachment to football brands. Williams (2007) comments that there is a relative lack of research into new international fandom, and that existing studies "have overly static ideas about the nature of fandom, which threaten, simply, to set up some familiar taxonomic sets ... for example: 'fans' against 'consumers'; TV fans against 'live' attenders'; 'traditional' supporters against 'new' fans (obviously, bad); and even 'hot' supporters 'cool' followers" (Giulianotti 2002).

Williams (2007) argues that there should be further consideration of what global fans might look like in the current age, without judging whether they are "good" or "bad."

One of the major developments that affects the way fans support their clubs lies in the area of technology. Internet literature points to the development of connected communities, whose sense of belonging, though carried out in the virtual world, may be just as real to them as in other types of communities. As far back as 1999, Kozinets talked about the creation of groups of people with similar interests who would form using the technology of the Internet. At this time there was little evidence that the Internet was creating this level of interaction, and a majority of its use was to display information or else to send e-mail.

Move forward ten years, however, and this seems entirely plausible. Indeed, examples abound of relationships instigated via the Internet, of gamers whose "Second Life" avatars take on so much reality for them that they enter into relationships, argue, and even kill in real life on the basis of the virtual characters that they have created and whose lives they enact. We may create and update Facebook identities to interact with our friends socially (even when we could meet physically or communicate via other media: for example, telephones), and social sites such as Twitter have become an accepted part of many people's lives.

In football terms, virtual fan communities develop around football web boards. So great is the sense of linkage between people within these communities that, even when they communicate using pseudonyms, they create a sense of belonging and shared purpose similar to that which might evolve in face-to-face communities. If this can happen locally, then there is no reason why these groups might not expand globally, or else separate subgroups might form in different locations around football teams.

These virtual communities and the way in which members demonstrate their membership is highlighted, for example, by Palmer and Thompson (2007), who talk about a group of South Australian football supporters known as the "Grog Squad."

These loyal fans of North Adelaide Australian Rules Football Club demonstrate belonging to this predominantly male social group through banter and practical jokes and a "mythology about alcohol-fuelled exploits," but the community goes far beyond this, offering access to a set of resources, benefits, and networks. Moreover, many of the rituals and behaviors that the authors describe as characterizing the "Grog Squad" also exist and are shared virtually via the Internet. The web board associated with the group at <www.rocketrooster.com>, The Roost, provides advice, information, and support on topics well outside of football. This is not unusual for football web boards, where communities share in each other's joys, sorrows, family events, and bereavements. The extent to which individuals will share with a group – a majority of whom they have never met – on the basis of an Internet connection seems to confound expectations. In some ways it might be easier to share feelings via the medium given the degree of anonymity that it offers. Also, the sense that those connected to the web board share a common passion seems to create a sense of unity and community among members.

CHAPTER 6

Managing football brands through different stages of the lifecycle

All brands evolve throughout their lifecycle. Even the most successful brands, such as Levi 501, experience highs and lows. For example, the Levi brand of jeans began to differentiate itself in the 1870s with a double line of stitching on the pockets, and the styles of its riveted jeans and leather badge were patented in the 1880s. The brand grew to great strength through the 1950s, but then suffered a decline in fortunes in the 1960s and 1970s, when jeans "became politicized through student protests" (Babson nd). The company briefly shifted its attention to products other than denim jeans, such as polyester suits, but in the 1980s built the Levi 501 brand to be a leading global brand. Since this time, the fortunes of Levi 501 have fluctuated with shifts in fashion preference among its youth market.

In the case of football brands, performance is clearly linked to the on-the-pitch performance of the particular club. So a football brand can grow in awareness and popularity if a team is successful, gains promotion, and membership of leagues for which there is greater TV coverage. In the English game, promotion to the Premier League offers a prize of around £60 million, in increased TV broadcast revenue, improved match attendance and merchandise sales. As a knock-on effect, promoted teams also come to the awareness of a much larger global audience, and their performance while in the league may gain them new fans who are attracted by their style of play, on-the-pitch success, or the players in the team.

Indeed, not only teams playing in the highest tier can gain significant international following: there are recent instances of clubs such as Stockport County of the English League One (third tier) and Sheffield United of the English Coca-Cola Championship (second tier) which have gained a significant following in China because of innovative brand expansion strategies.

Stockport County, for example, capitalized on the popularity of English football as a whole by undertaking close season tours in China, and building a local fan base and an eventual joint venture with a local club.

Sheffield United has linked up with international clubs both in Hungary (Ferencváros) and in China (Chengdu Blades) to create feeder clubs and also to boost international interest in its brand.

The nature of sport, however, and the reason fans become so passionate about their clubs, is that it is never clear what the result will be in a particular match. For the good times, there are inevitably less successful periods of time.

The following section discusses what constitutes "success" in football brands.

What are successful football brands?

Success for a football brand surely relates to winning silverware and leagues. Yet, if that were the only criteria for success, fans of many league clubs would not have experienced any success in their lifetime.

Actual success in football relates to final league positions and winning matches. In some cases this also translates into financial benefits to clubs. So, for example, in the Spanish league system, more successful teams tend to negotiate better broadcast deals. Teams that qualify for the European Champions League or equivalent competitions gain greater gate receipts and broadcast revenue, which they can reinvest in better players. So begins a virtual cycle of success. Statistically, teams with better playing squads (as measured by average wages of the players) achieve better sporting performance (Deloitte and Touche 2009). Rich clubs tend to get richer, and the gap between successful and less successful clubs tends to perpetuate over time.

There are, however, other measures of success for football clubs. Despite high levels of sporting performance, there are clubs that, for reasons of geography, may not attract high attendances. For example, Scunthorpe United FC was promoted in 2008–09 to the English Coca-Cola Championship (second tier). When it was last in the second tier, it sold 4,000 season tickets in advance of the season. By June 2009 it had only sold 2,700 tickets (BBC: http://news.bbc.co.uk/sport1/hi/football/teams/s/scunthorpe_utd/8117287.stm), probably as a result of the difficult economic climate. Newcastle United, which will also be playing in the second tier in 2009–10, had sold 25,000 season tickets. Economists tend to use both average attendance and variability of attendance (difference between the highest and lowest attendance) as measures of success in football clubs (Baade and Tiehen 1990). These translate in turn to revenue, so the logic for including a measure of attendance is clear.

Another interesting phenomenon in football is that fans may perceive levels of success that are different from the actual level of success of the club. If a team exceeds the level of performance that is expected of it (for example, Stoke City and Hull City in reaching the Premier League and remaining in the league in 2008–09), its fans evaluate its levels of success as high. The fans of teams that tend always to achieve high levels of performance, such as Arsenal (fourth) and Chelsea (third), might evaluate their team as having been relatively unsuccessful even though the actual level of performance was considerably higher than that of either Stoke City (12th) or Hull (17th). The perceptual nature of success in football can be challenging for football clubs.

Success must be *continual* and *progressive* in order to meet the expectations of fans.

In 1999–2000 and 2000–01, Sunderland AFC, which was typically a club that yo-yoed between the Premier League and Championship (first and second tiers of English football), achieved two successive seventh-place finishes under the stewardship of Peter Reid. This achievement, with a relatively modest player budget, was a massive over-achievement for the club at that time. As soon as the club gained safety – at that time about 40 points for the season – fans began to discuss the chances of qualifying for European competition. Indeed many fans complained that the board was showing a lack of ambition in not building upon this level of success by buying players capable of moving the club on to the next level. When the club eventually did buy a set of more expensive players in 2001–02, this was not enough to save it from relegation. The gap in revenue between the Premier League and Championship was even then (and it is larger now, although thankfully so are also the parachute payments to relegated clubs by the Premier League) so great that the club had to sell more than a squad's worth of players in order to readjust its finances to the lower level.

The challenges of building for success in football are in many cases greater than those facing clubs in difficult times. To what extent should the club speculate and expand its squad size and improve the quality of its players? How does the club respond – particularly in times when there is a buoyant player transfer market – to the difficulties of attracting top players to clubs that are not at the highest level? This can sometimes require higher transfer fees and better personal terms than the player might get from a more established club. Some leagues have caps for player wages – this type of cap now exists in the Bundesliga, and player wages are also controlled in US Major League Soccer, as well as in English League Two (the fourth tier of English football). In other cases, clubs must decide on the extent to which they are prepared to speculate and commit resources to try to reach the prize of greater sporting performance.

Examples such as that of Leeds United in the early 2000s serve as a cautionary tale to clubs that are tempted to borrow too greatly (overgear) to achieve this. Having achieved Champions League qualification in 1999–2000, Leeds United narrowly missed out in 2000–01 (when it finished in fourth place, one spot outside Champions League qualification), and in 2001–02 (when it finished in fifth place). In the attempt to qualify for the Champions League for the sporting and financial benefits, the club had borrowed heavily. Although in many ways the club was unlucky – had the player transfer market not also hit a decline at this time, it could presumably have sold its more expensive and higher paid players at a profit, and this might have resolved the issues of high interest rates on its loans – its resultant financial problems showed the dangers of stretching too far. After having to sell its players to try to avoid financial meltdown, the club was eventually relegated at the end of the 2003–04 season. It narrowly missed promotion back to the Premier League, losing to Watford in the play-off final in 2005–06, but then went into administration at the end of the 2006–07 season, after already being relegated to League One (the third tier).

Leadership literature identifies a number of different contexts and challenges for leaders in organizations. For example Leavy and Wilson (1994) identify four types of leadership challenges in organizations:

- **Builders:** Tend to be building for the first time. In football terms, this might be the challenges facing a club that builds from the bottom of the non-league pyramid, or one that enters the professional league for the first time.
- **Turnarounders:** There is significant rebuilding to be undertaken. This might be the situation if a club has been relegated, or even if, as in the Leeds United example above, the club has had successive relegations. The challenges may involve a large number of player sales, and purchase of new players suited to the current status of the club.
- **Revitalizers:** Less dramatic change is needed here. This might be the case for a club that just missed out on promotion, has spent several years in a particular division, and is trying to work out what it needs to do differently and change in order to build to the next level.
- **Inheritors:** This is the situation when a club is already successful, but for various reasons, the baton must be passed on to a next generation. In leadership terms, this would be the case as and when Sir Alex Ferguson retires as manager of Manchester United and a new manager must come in and continue the success in their own style but without doing anything to jeopardize that success.

Wilson and Leavy's categories are based on studies of a broader range of organizations, but seem to capture many of the challenges facing football clubs. These same challenges apply not only to the managers of the clubs (see Bridgewater 2010, *Football Management,* for more detail on the on-the-pitch challenges in football), but also to the custodians of these football brands.

When applied to football brand management, the primary marketing challenges of each of these situations might be summed up as follows.

Building football brands

Whether a club is newly formed or has moved to a completely different stage of its development, the challenges here are akin to those facing new products of services. Following the AIDA model of consumer behavior (Awareness, Interest, Desire, and Action), or "hierarchy of effects" (Lavidge and Steiner 1961), marketers have to build *awareness* that the club exists, communicate positive messages to potential fans about the benefits of being involved, perhaps create *trial* (getting someone who has not previously been interested in football to engage with the sport) by hosting events for children, playing a high-profile friendly match, or otherwise gaining the *interest* of potential fans, sponsors, and the other stakeholders who will be essential to future success. The media might also play a valuable role in communicating the brand values of this club: what does it stand for? What is distinctive about it that might attract fans? Having established why fans might *desire* to attend matches and become involved, the fan must then be persuaded to act on this and attend a match, and subsequently become a repeat attendee. As described in Chapter 2, consumer behavior describes this process of moving a consumer towards purchase as going through a series of stages (Palda 1966):

- Cognitive brand awareness, recognition, and recall
- Affective attitude towards, liking of, and preference for one among alternatives
- Conative intention to buy.

Turnaround

If a football club has gone through difficult times, on or off the pitch, the challenges will not only be those of rebuilding the team and rebuilding sporting success, but may also include rebuilding interest and confidence in the club. As shown at the beginning of this chapter, it is certainly not uncommon for brands to experience difficult times. Young and Rubicam, in presenting its Brand Asset Valuator (BAV) framework, show brand value as being based on brand vitality (differentiation and relevance) and brand stature (esteem and knowledge). A brand might become less successful if it loses either brand vitality or brand stature.

So, for example, in the 1990s, AB's Budweiser targeted 18–24-year-old males in the United States, but spent some of its money in promoting concerts by the Rolling Stones. Over time Budweiser had become perceived as less relevant to the younger market and as being "Dad's beer." This would be a loss of *relevance*, similar to that experienced by Marks & Spencer, whose appeal over some years seemed to age with its core market.

A brand might also lose its *differentiation* – whatever makes it stand out from other brands. In football terms, this happens if a key player leaves, or if sporting performance declines.

A loss of *esteem* would occur if a brand lost its emotional appeal to its customers. This tends to happen long after a loss of relevance or differentiation. Emotional bonds are difficult to break. There was still goodwill towards Marks & Spencer during its difficult times, even among people who were no longer buying goods from the store. In football terms, this might be the case if fans decided not to attend matches or renew a season ticket because of poor performance, but were still emotionally attached to the club and constituted a group of fans who could be wooed back.

Knowledge is simply awareness of the brand. If the club takes positive actions, for example signs new players, reduces the price of its season tickets, or otherwise revises its offer to make it more attractive, it needs to make all efforts to make its fans aware of its actions in order to reap rewards.

Revitalizing football brands

It may be that there is nothing that needs radical overhaul at a club, but that it needs to move on to the next level. This might, for example, be a realization that the club needs to find additional investment in order to build a new stadium. An urge to revitalize has recently been expressed by Bill Kenwright, chairman of Everton Football Club, who told a shareholders' EGM in September 2008 that he felt the time was right for Everton to find a "billionaire" investor who would be able to take the club on to the next level. The club has performed consistently well and above expectation under manager David Moyes, but the takeover of Manchester City by the Abu Dhabi United Group prompted Kenwright's concern that the financial requirements to gain success in the English Premier League were moving from the preserve of millionaires to billionaires.

Revitalizing of football brands (as with turnaround) may often – but is not always – associated with new investment or new owners. It may simply be that a club has areas in which it would like to strengthen its brand. These could be in any of the areas identified in the previous section, but may not require such radical changes as in turnaround.

Inheriting football brands

Nothing fails like success. In many ways one of the biggest challenges for a marketer is to take over a brand that is successful and to continue to manage this success. Successful brands continually innovate and look for ways to be different or better than competitors. This may mean breaking up a successful team and bringing in new or younger players at the right time so that the team does not begin to age and lose its edge.

When football brands do badly

The title of this section is adapted from a well-known marketing article by Jennifer Aaker and colleagues (2004), "When good brands do bad." For most types of brands, Aaker shows that, if the brand performs badly, a customer will consider switching to a different brand. If I bought a certain type of computer once, and it went wrong rapidly, I might view this as unfortunate. If it happened twice I would probably buy a different type of computer the next time (if I did not do so after the first time). Brand switching rarely happens in football, though, and never happens among fans with attitudinal loyalty. It may occasionally happen among children who are still developing their particular allegiance, or among fans who enjoy football as a sporting spectacle but are not particularly affiliated to a team. For most fans, the idea that if Newcastle United lost a match their fans would switch allegiance to Sunderland, Arsenal fans to Tottenham, AC Milan to Inter Milan, and so on, is totally unimaginable.

How then do football fans respond when times are hard? What is the reaction that they show instead of switching? As was mentioned in Chapter 2, Cialdini and colleagues (1976) suggest that football fans externalize poor performance, while they internalize good performance. Cialdini describes these behaviors as:

- bask in reflected glory (BIRG) when things are going well, but
- cut off rejected failure (CORF) if things go badly.

Part of this rejection of failure is to externalize, or put the blame, for poor performance on someone else, although fans tend to take credit for success. "We raised the roof and intimidated the opposition," but *they* (manager, referee, board, players) should have done something to stop us from losing. This makes it great to be a fan, but intensely frustrating to be a football marketer, manager, or match official!

In addition to apportioning blame, football fans may find poor performance too difficult to handle, and tend to distance themselves if this is too painful. It is not uncommon that a fan will decide not to go out socially after a loss, or will avoid looking at websites and newspapers that they would read in great detail after a victory.

What then are the possible strategies for a football marketer when football performance is poor? Thankfully football matches come thick and fast. Even a resounding defeat might best be addressed by victory in the next match. Where a run of poor results builds fan dissatisfaction, clubs might focus on the broader aspects of being a fan. Some reasons for support of clubs are about success. Others, however, are about belonging, shared history, and the broader role of the club.

Of course turning around performance is the best, and preferred option. In the short term, however, fans might appreciate the club's activities in the community, opportunities to give their views, and other communication from the club, good performances from individuals, and the bigger picture generally. It may be that the club is making the first step on a long journey, whereby it needs to adjust its wage bill or bring through younger players. While all fans are impatient for success, most fans are realistic when reminded that a club may be new into a division, may not have the budget of some rivals, and is bringing through young players, or other rational arguments that counter the immediate emotional response.

Moreover fans play a role in success. Some fans defend their right to heckle players on the "I pay my money, I am entitled to behave how I want and say what I want" basis. While this is true – within reason – there is no doubting that the chances of a striker who is lacking in confidence, or a player who missed a penalty kick last time round scoring with his next, are unlikely to be improved by abuse from the crowd. A majority of fans will appreciate that their positive behavior and its benefits for the players may help to break rather than to perpetuate the crisis.

Final comments

Some readers will have felt – probably from the moment that they first saw the title of this book – a strong antipathy to the notion that football teams, clubs, individual players, and sporting bodies should be viewed as brands. This is seen by some as a betrayal of the beautiful game, of the pure sporting ideals of the game of football. Football, they argue, is spoilt by commercialization. If clubs can buy success, then the essence of the game will be ruined. There are indeed causes for concern in the commercialization of football. For example, if the gap between the leagues becomes so big that promoted teams ruin their longer-term finances in the attempt to stay in the league, then the future of football is at risk. If rich clubs continue to get richer to the extent that competitive balance within and between leagues is destroyed, and the same few teams win the leagues in their country every year, if underdogs never go on cup runs, if the form book is never overturned, then football will really have killed the goose that lays the golden egg.

Despite these concerns, and a – perhaps understandable – nostalgia for a bygone era of football, most would agree that it is impossible now to turn back the clock on the commercialization of football. Also, we might remember that in the simpler age of football, stadia were often lacking in basic amenities, and crowd safety was a much greater concern.

Commercial development of football is here to stay. Expressions such as "unprecedented" or "outstanding" growth and "relentless" progress can be seen throughout recent Deloitte and Touche annual reviews of football finance. Alongside any concerns that it might provoke, commercial growth has also attracted into the game a rising generation of sporting stars. A number of stars of other sports first tried their hand at football, but having been unsuccessful, went on to be Olympic athletes and big success stories in other sports. Such is the appeal of football, and this comes – in part – from the high rewards that have come with commercial growth.

Despite the negative feelings that some fans may have about viewing football clubs, stars, or football bodies and competitions as brands, brands are not always about commercialization – there are many brands for charities and public sector organizations – because the true meaning of marketing is understanding the needs and wants of those people who are involved with that particular organization.

The focus in this book on football brands allows us to look through a different lens. This lens helps us to understand:

- what fans find attractive or unattractive in a club
- what makes fans want to watch football or attend matches
- what builds loyalty to a club
- what might be improved
- what helps to sustain loyalty when teams perform badly.

Football brands are unique. Football clubs, stars, and the game itself are unique. There is a level of emotional involvement between fans and football which makes the thirst for understanding of their clubs and the game second to none. It is the extraordinary loyalty of football fans, often through the hard times, which makes football brands unique, and this book is dedicated to the fans of football who make the game the success that it is. This book is as much for marketers in other fields, who can learn from looking at football brands and the challenges they face, as for football fans, without whom there would be no football brands.

References

Aaker, D. A. (1991) *Managing Brand Equity*, New York, Free Press.

Aaker, D. (1996) *Building Strong Brands*, New York, Free Press.

Aaker, D. (2004) "Leveraging the corporate brand," in *California Management Review*, 46(3), 618.

Aaker, J. L. (1997) "Dimensions of brand personality," *Journal of Marketing Research,* 34(3) (August), 347–56.

Aaker, J. L., Fournier, S. M., and Brasel, S. A. (2004) "When good brands do bad," *Journal of Consumer Research,* 31(June), 1–16.

American Marketing Association (AMA) (1960) *Marketing Definitions: A glossary of marketing terms*, Chicago, Ill., AMA.

Andrews, I. (1998) "The transformation of a community in the Australian football league. Part one: Towards a conceptual framework for the community," *Occasional Papers in Football Studies,* 1(2), 103–14.

Andrews, L. (2006) "Spin: from tactic to tabloid," *Journal of Public Affairs,* 6(1) (February), 31–45.

Baade, R. A. and Tiehen, L. J. (1990) "The impact of stadiums and professional sports on metropolitan area development," *Growth and Change,* 21, 1–14.

Babson College (nd) Case 148-C97A "Not by jeans alone: the story of Levi's," http://faculty.babson.edu/wylie/CRR1/148c97a.pdf (accessed February 11, 2010).

Backman, S. J. and Crompton, J. L. (1991) "The usefulness of selected variables for predicting activity loyalty," *Leisures Sciences*, 13, 205–20.

Bainbridge, J. (1997) "Coke nets chief for soccer post," *Marketing,* 2.

Baker, J. and Cameron, M. (1996) "The effects of service environment on affect and consumer perception of waiting time: an integrative review and research propositions," *Journal of the Academy of Marketing Science*, 24(4), 338–49.

Bale, J. (1994) *Landscapes of Sport,* Leicester, Leicester University Press.

Berry, L., Carbone, L., and Haeckel, S. (2002) "Managing the total customer experience," *MIT Sloan Management Review,* 43(3), 85–9.

Bitner, M. J. (1992) "Servicescapes: the impact of physical surroundings and employee responses," *Journal of Marketing*, 56(2), 57–71.

Bitran, G. R., Ferrer, J.-C. and Oliveira, P. R. (2008) "Managing customer experiences: perspectives on the temporal aspects of service encounters," *Manufacturing Service Operations Management*, 10(1), 61–83.

Blackshaw, T. (2008) "Contemporary community theory and football," *Soccer and Society*, 9(3), 325–45.

Bolt, R. (1966) *A Man for all Seasons*, London, Heinemann.

Bose, M. (2007) *Manchester Disunited: And the Business of Soccer*, London, Arum.

Boulding, K. (1956), *The Image*, Ann Arbor, Mich., University of Michigan Press.

Brand Finance (2009) "The power of brands: the most valuable European football brands 2009," *Soccerex Business*, Q1, 18.

Branscombe, N. R. and Wann, D. L. (1992) "Role of identification with a group, arousal, categorization processes, and self-esteem in sports spectator aggression," *Human Relations*, 45(10), 1013.

Branscombe, N. R. and Wann, D. (1994) "Sport psychology," in *Magill's Survey of Social Sciences: Psychology*, 2363–8.

Bridgewater, S (2004) "Perceptions of the England national football brand in China," working paper, Warwick Business School.

Bridgewater, S. and Stray, S. (2002) "Brand values in professional sports: Premiership football clubs in the UK," in *Proceedings of the European Marketing Academy Conference, Braga, Portugal*.

Bristow, D. and Sebastian, R. (2001) "Holy cow! Wait 'til next year! A closer look at the brand loyalty of Chicago Cubs baseball fans," *Journal of Consumer Marketing*, 18(3), 256–75.

Bromberger, C. (ed.) (1998) *Passions ordinaires: du match de football au concours de dictée*, Paris, Bayard.

Brown, A. (2004) "Manchester is red? Manchester United, fan identity and the 'sport city,'" in D Andrews (ed.), *Manchester United: A thematic study*, London, Routledge.

Brown, A. (2008) "Our club, our rules: fan communities at FC United of Manchester," *Soccer and Society,* 9(3): 346–58.

Brown, A., Crabbe, T., and Mellor, G. (2006) *Football and its Communities: Final Report for the Football Foundation*, London, Football Foundation.

Brown, A., Crabbe, T., and Mellor, G. (eds) (2009) *Football and*

Community in the Global Context: Studies in theory and practice, London, Routledge.

Buzzell, R. D. (1968) "Can you standardize multinational marketing?" *Harvard Business Review*, November–December, 102–13.

Carlyle, T. (1889) *On Heroes, Hero-Worship and the Heroic Ideal in History*, London, Chapman & Hall.

Cialdini, R. B., Borden, R. J., Thorne, A., Wilker, M. R., Freeman, S., and Sloan, L. R. (1976) "Basking in reflected glory: three (football) studies," *Journal of Personal and Social Psychology*, 34, 366–75.

Coffin, T. P. and Cohen, H. (1978) *The Parade of Heroes: Legendary figures in American lore*, New York, Doubleday.

Cohen, A. (1985) *The Symbolic Construction of Community*, London, Tavistock.

Collier, D.A. (1994) *The Service/Quality Solution: Using service management to gain competitive advantage*, Burr Ridge, Ill., Quality Press and Richard D. Irwin.

Cova, B. (1997) "Community and consumption: towards a definition of the 'linking value' of product or services," *European Journal of Marketing*, 31(3/4), 297–316.

Davenport, T. and Beck, J. (2002) *The Attention Economy: Understanding the new currency of business,* Boston, Mass., Harvard Business School Press.

Davidson, H. (1998) *Even More Offensive Marketing,* London, Penguin.

Day, G. S. (1969) "A two-dimensional concept of brand loyalty," *Journal of Advertising Research*, 9, 29–35.

De Chernatony, L. (2001) *From Brand Vision to Brand Evaluation: Strategically building and sustaining brands,* Oxford, Butterworth-Heinemann.

De Chernatony, L. and McDonald, M. (1998) *Creating Powerful Brands in Consumer, Service and Industrial Markets*, Oxford, Butterworth-Heinemann.

Deloitte and Touche (2009) *Annual Review of Football Finance.*

Department of Communities and Local Government (2000) *Our Towns and Cities: The Future –Delivering an Urban Renaissance,* November 16 [online] http://www.communities.gov.uk/publications/citiesandregions/ourtowns (accessed February 11, 2010).

Desbordes, M. (ed.) (2007) *Marketing and Football: An international perspective,* Oxford, Butterworth-Heinemann.

Dick, A. S. and Basu, K. (1994) "Customer loyalty: towards an integrated conceptual framework," *Journal of Academy of Marketing Science*, 22(2) (Fall), 99–113.

Domazlicky, B. R. and Kerr, P. M. (1990) "Baseball attendance and the designated hitter," *American Economist,* 34, 62–8.

Douglas, S. and Wind, Y. (1987) "The myth of globalization," *Columbia Journal of World Business* (Winter), 19–29.

Doyle, P (2002) *Marketing Management and Strategy,* 3rd edn, Harlow, FT Prentice Hall.

Dunning, E., Murphy, P., and Williams, J. (1986) "Spectator violence at football matches: towards a sociological explanation," *British Journal of Sociology*, 37, 221–44.

Eon (2009) *Origins of Support,* research findings.

Financial Times (1991) "Price to book ratio of brand name stocks," November 23, p. 111.

Foer, F. (2004). *How Soccer Explains the World: An unlikely theory of globalization,* New York, HarperCollins.

Football Task Force (1999) "Football: commercial issues," submission by the Football Task Force to the Minister for Sport, December 22, 1999.

Forbes Magazine (2007) "The world's top sports brands," September 29.

Forbes Magazine (2008) "The world's best paid soccer players," April 30.

Frey, J. H. (1992) "Gambling on sport: policy issues," *Journal of Gambling Studies*, 8, 351–60.

Fullerton, S. (1995) "An application of market segmentation in a sports marketing arena: we can't all be Greg Norman," *Sport Marketing Quarterly,* 4(3), 43–7.

Funk, D. C. and James, J. (2001) "The psychological continuum model: a conceptual framework for understanding an individual's psychological connection to sport," *Sport Management Review*, 4(2), 119–50.

Gantz, W. (1981) "An exploration of viewing motives and behavious associated with television sports," *Journal of Broadcasting,* 25(3), 263–75.

Gantz, W. and Wenner, L. A. (1995) "Fanship and the television sports viewing experience," *Sociology of Sport Journal*, 12, 56–74.

Gibson, H., Willming, G., and Holdnak, A. (2002) "We're Gators ... not just Gator fans: serious leisure and University of Florida football," *Journal of Leisure Research*, 34, 397–426.

Giddens, A. (1998) *The Third Way: The renewal of social democracy*, Cambridge, Polity.

Giddens, A. (1994) *Beyond Left and Right: The future of radical politics*, Stanford, Calif., Stanford University Press.

Gilfeather, P. (2002). "27million: that's how much David Blunkett has spent on spin in just one year," *Daily Mirror,* January 8.

Giulianotti, R. (1999) *Football: A sociology of the modern game*, Cambridge, Polity Press.

Giulianotti, R. (2002) "Supporters, followers, fans and flaneurs: a taxonomy of spectator identities in football," *Journal of Sport and Social Issues*, 29(4), 386–410.

Giulianotti, R. (2007) "Forms of glocalization: globalization and the migration strategies of Scottish football fans in North America" *Sociology,* 4 (February), 133–52.

Giulianotti, R. and Robertson, R. (2004) "The globalization of football: a study in the glocalization of the serious life," *British Journal of Sociology,* 55(4), 545–68.

Gladden, J. M. and Funk, D. C. (2001) "Understanding brand loyalty in professional sport: examining the link between brand associations and brand loyalty," *International Journal of Sports Marketing and Sponsorship*, 3(1), 67–94.

Gobé, M. and Zyman, S. (2001) *Emotional Branding: The new paradigm for connecting brands to people*, New York, Allworth Press.

Haley, R. I. (1968) "Benefit segmentation: a decision-oriented research tool," *Journal of Marketing,* July, 21–32.

Hamel, G. and Prahalad, C. K. (1985) "Do you really have a global strategy?" *Harvard Business Review,* July–August, 139–48.

Harris, F. and de Chernatonay, L. (2001) "Corporate branding and corporate brand performance," *European Journal of Marketing,* 35(3/4), 441–56.

Holt, R. (1989) *Sport and the British: A modern history,* Oxford, Oxford University Press.

Home Office (1989) *The Taylor Report: The Hillsborough Stadium Disaster*, April 15, London, HMSO.

Hopkins, G (2010) *Star-Spangled Soccer,* Basingstoke, Palgrave Macmillan.

Hornby, N. (1992) *Fever Pitch*, London, Penguin.

Hout, T., Porter, M. E., and Rudden, E. (1985) "How global companies win out," *Harvard Business Review,* September–October, 98–108.

Hughes-Hallett, L. (2004) *Heroes: Saviours, traitors and supermen*, London, Fourth Estate.

Hughson, J. (2009a) "On sporting heroes," *Sport in Society*, 12(1), 85–101.

Hughson, J. (2009b) "The modern city and the making of sport," *Sport in Society*, 12(1), 102–17.

Hui, M. K. and Bateson, J. E. (1991) "Perceived control and consumer choice on the service experience," *Journal of Consumer Research*, 18, 174–85.

Iggulden, C. and Iggulden, D. (2009) *The Dangerous Book of Heroes*, London, Harper Collins.

Independent Football Commission (IFC) (2004) *Annual Report*, London, IFC.

Inglis, S. (1990) *The Football Grounds of Europe*, London, Willow/ Collins.

Jacoby, J. and Chestnut, R. W. (1978) *Brand Loyalty Measurement and Management*, New York, Wiley.

Jensen, R. (1999). *The Dream Society: How the coming shift from information to imagination will transform your business*, New York, McGraw-Hill.

Johnson, G. and Scholes, K. (1992) *Exploring Corporate Strategy*, 3rd edn, Englewood Cliffs, N.J., Prentice-Hall.

Kahle, L. R., Kambara, K. M., and Rose, G. M. (1996) "A functional model of fan attendance, motivations for college football," *Sport Marketing Quarterly*, 5(4), 51–60.

Kapferer, J.-N. (1997) *Strategic Brand Management*, London, Kogan Page.

Keller, K. (1993) "Conceptualizing, measuring and managing customer-based brand equity," *Journal of Marketing*, 57(1), 1–22.

Keller, K. (2001) "Building customer-based brand equity," *Marketing Management*, July/August: 15–19.

Koerning, S. K. and Boyd, T. C. (2009) "To catch a tiger or let him go: the match-up effect and athlete endorsers for sport and non-sports brands," *Sport Marketing Quarterly*, 18, 25–37.

Koo, G.-Y. and Hardin, R. (2008) "Difference in interrelationship between spectators' motives and behavioral intentions based on emotional attachment," *Sport Marketing Quarterly*, 17(1), 30–43.

Kozinets, R.V. (1999) "E-tribalized marketing: the strategic implications," *European Management Journal*, 17(3), 252–64.

Kumar, A. and Oliver, R. L. (1997) "Cognitive appraisals, consumer emotions, and consumer response," *Advances in Consumer Research*, 24(1), 17–18.

Langmeyer, L. and Shank, M. D. (1993) "Celebrity endorsers and public service agencies: a balancing act," in E. Thorson (ed.), *Proceedings of the 1993 Conference at the Academy of Advertising,* 197–207.

Lascu, D.-N., Giese, T. D., Toolan, M. S. M., Guehring, B., and Mercer, J. (1995) "Sport involvement: a relevant individual difference factor in spectator sports," *Sport Marketing Quarterly,* 4(4), 41–7.

Lavidge, R. C. and Steiner, G. A. (1961) "A model for prediction measurements of advertising effectiveness," *Journal of Marketing*, 25 (October), 59–62.

Leavy, B. and Wilson, D. C. (1994) *Strategy and Leadership*, London, Routledge.

Levitt, T. (1983) "The globalization of markets," *Harvard Business Review*, May–June, 92–102.

Lorenz, C. (1985) "The birth of a transnational," *McKinsey Quarterly,* Autumn, 72–93.

Maffesoli, M. (1996) *The Time of the Tribes: The decline of individualism in mass society*, London, Sage.

Madrigal, R. (1995) "Cognitive and affective determinants of fan satisfaction with sporting event attendance," *Journal of Leisure Research*, 27(3), 205–27.

Mahony, D. F., Madrigal, R., and Howard, D. R. (1999) "The effect of self-monitoring on behavioural and attitudinal loyalty towards athletic teams," *International Journal of Sport Marketing and Sponsorship*, 1. 146–67.

Mahony, D. F., Madrigal, R., and Howard, D. (2000) "Using the Psychological Commitment to Team (PCT) scale to segment sport consumers based on loyalty," *Sport Marketing Quarterly*, 9(1), 15–25.

Mahony, D. F., Nakazawa, M., Funk, D., James, J. D., and Gladden, J. M. (2002) "Motivational factors influencing the behaviour of J. League spectators," *Sport Management Review*, 5, 1–24.

McCracken, G. (1989) "Who is the celebrity endorser? Cutural foundations of the endorsement process," *Journal of Consumer Research*, 16(3), 310–21.

McPherson, B. (1975) "Sport consumption and the economics of consumerism," in D. W. Ball and J. W. Loy (eds), *Sport and Social Order: Contributions to the sociology of sport*, Reading, Mass., Addison-Wesley, 243–75.

Mehrabian, A. and Russell, J. (1974) *An Approach to Environmental*

Psychology, Cambridge, Mass., Massachusetts Institute of Psychology.

Mellor, G. (2008) "The Janus-faced sport: English football, community and the legacy of the 'third way,'" *Soccer and Society*, 9(3), 313–24.

Melnick, M. J. (1993) "Searching for sociability in the stands: a theory of sports spectating," *Journal of Sport Management*, 7, 44–60.

Moore, K (1997) *Museums and Popular Culture,* London, Cassell.

Mumford, L. (1938) *The Culture of Cities*, London, Martin Secker & Warburg.

Newman, P. and Tual, M. (2002) "The Stade de France: the last expression of French centralism?" *European Planning Studies*, 10(7), 831.

Ohmae, K. (1985) *The Borderless World*, London, Collins.

Oliver, R. L. (1997) *Satisfaction: A behavioral perspective on the consumer*, New York, McGraw-Hill.

O'Neil, T. (2006) *The Men in Black: Inside Manchester United's football hooligan gang*, Manchester, Milon.

Ozanian, M. K. (2005) "The business of soccer," *Forbes*, January 4, 25–34.

Palda, K. S. (1966) "The hypothesis of a hierarchy of effects," *Journal of Marketing Research*, 3(1), 13–24.

Palmer, C. and Thompson, K. (2007) "The paradoxes of football spectatorship: on-field and online expressions of social capital among the grog squad," *Sociology of Sport Journal*, 24, 187–205.

Perrier, R (ed.) (1997) *Brand Valuation,* London, Premier Books.

Petkus, E. Jr. (2004) "Enhancing the application of experiential marketing in the arts," *International Journal of Nonprofit and Voluntary Sector Marketing*, 9, 49–56.

Pine, J. P. and Gilmore, J. H. (1999) *The Experience Economy*, Boston, Mass., Harvard Business School Press.

Prisuta, R. H. (1979) "Televised sports and political values," *Journal of Communication*, 29, 94–102.

Pullman, M. E. and Gross, M. A. (2004) "Ability of experience design elements to elicit emotions and loyalty behaviours," *Decision Sciences*, 35(3), 531–76.

Quelch, J. A. and Hoff, E. J. (1986) "Customising global marketing," *Harvard Business Review*, May–June: 59–68.

Quick, S. and Van Leuwen, L. (1998) "'Winning, is it the only thing?' Contributing elements in a fan's decision to consume professional sport," paper presented at the ANZSA Conference, December, Melbourne.

Reichheld, F. (1997) "The bottom line on customer loyalty," *Management Review*, 86(3) (March), 16.

Reichheld, F., Markey, R. G., and Hopton, C. (2000) "The loyalty effect – the relationship between loyalty and profits," *European Business Journal,* 12(3), 134.

Ries, A. and Trout, J. (1986) *Positioning: The battle for your mind,* New York, McGraw-Hill.

Riesenbeck, H. and Freeling, A. (1991) "How global are global brands?" *McKinsey Quarterly*, 4, 3–18.

Riess, S. A. (1991) *City Games: The evolution of American urban society and the rise of sports,* Urbana, Ill., University of Illinois Press.

Rugman, A. M. (1986) "New theories of the multinational enterprise: an assessment of internalization theory," *Bulletin of Economic Research*, 38(2), 101–18.

Russell, D. (1997) *Football and the English: A social history of Association Football in England, 1863–1995*, Preston, Carnegie.

Schimmel, K. S. (2001) "Sport matters: urban regime theory and urban regeneration in the late capitalist era," in C. Gratton and I. P. Henry (eds), *Sport in the City: The role of sport in economic and social regeneration*, London, Routledge, 259–77.

Schroeder, A. (2004) *Celebrity-in-Chief: How show business took over the White House,* Oxford,Westview Press.

Sebastian, R. J. and Bristow, D. N. (2000) "Win or lose, take me out to the ball game! An empirical investigation of loyalty proneness among college students," *Sport Marketing Quarterly*, 9(4), 211–20.

Sheth, J. N. (1987) "A normative theory of marketing practice," in G. Frazier and N. Sheth (eds), *Contemporary Views of Marketing Practice,* Lexington, Mass., Lexington Press, 19–31.

Sloan, L. R. (1989) "The motives of sports fans," in J. D. Goldstein (ed.), *Sports, Games and Play: Social and psychosocial viewpoints*, 2nd edn, Hilldown, N.J., Lawrence Erlbaum, 175–240.

Smith, G. J. (1988) "The noble sports fan," *Journal of Sports and Social Issues*, 12, 54–65.

Soccerex Business (2009) Quarter 1.

Stewart, R. and Smith, A. (1997) "Sports watching in Australia: a theoretical and empirical overview," in *Advancing Sports Management in Australia and New Zealand, SKAANZ Annual Conference*

Proceedings, Auckland, 1–32.

Supporters Direct (2005) *Evidence to the FA Structural Review*, London, Supporters Direct.

Sutton, W. A., McDonald, M. A., Milne, G. R., and Cimperman, J. (1997) "Creating and fostering fan identification in professional sports," *Sport Marketing Quarterly,* 6(1), 15–22.

Tacon, R. (2007) "Football and social inclusion: evaluating social policy," *Managing Leisure*, 12(1) (January), 1–23.

Tapp, A. (2004) "The loyalty of football fans – we'll support you ever-more?" *Database Marketing and Customer Strategy Management*, 11(3), 203–15.

Tapp, A. and Clowes, J. (2002) "From 'carefree casuals' to professional wanderers': segmentation possibilities for football supporters," *European Journal of Marketing,* 36 (11/12), 1248–69.

Thornley, A. (2002) "Urban regeneration and sports stadia," *European Planning Studies*, 10(7), 813–18.

Thurow, R. (1997) "To see why the NFL still thrives, consider Jersey John's Odysseys," *Wall Street Journal,* October 10.

Toffler, A. (1970) *Future Shock,* New York, Bantam.

Turner, V. (1969) *The Ritual Process: Structure and anti-structure,* London, Routledge.

Underwood, R., Bond, E., and Baer, R. (2001) "Building service brands via social identity: lessons from the sports marketplace," *Journal of Marketing Theory and Practice,* Winter, 1–12.

Wagg, S. (2004) "Fat city? British football and the politics of social exclusion at the turn of the twenty-first century," in S. Wagg (ed.), *British Football and Social Exclusion*, London, Routledge.

Wakefield, K. (1995) "The pervasive influence of social influence on sporting event attendance," *Journal of Sport and Social Issues*, 19, 377–96.

Wakefield, K. L. and Blodgett, J. G. (1994) "The importance of servic-escapes in leisure service settings," *Journal of Services Marketing*, 8(3), 66–76.

Wakefield, K. and Blodgett, G. (1996) "The effect of the servicescape on customers' behavioral intentions in leisure service settings," *Journal of Services Marketing*, 10(6), 45–61.

Wakefield, K. L. and Sloan, H. J. (1995) "The effects of team loyalty and selected stadium factors on spectator attendance," *Journal of Sport Management,* 19, 153–72.

Wakefield, K. L. and Wann, D. (2006) "An examination of

dysfunctional sports fans: method of classification and relationships with problem behaviours," *Journal of Leisure Research*, 38(2), 168–86.

Wann, D. (1994) "The 'noble' sports fan: the relationships between team identification, self-esteem and aggression," *Perceptual and Motor Skills,* 78, 864–6.

Wann, D. L. (1995) "Preliminary validation of the Sport Fan Motivation Scale," *Journal of Sport and Social Issues*, 19, 377–96.

Wann, D. and Branscombe, N. R. (1993) "Sports fans: measuring degree of identification with their team," *International Journal of Sport Psychology,* 24, 1–17.

Wann, D. and Dolan, T. J. (2001) "Attributions of highly identified sports spectators," *Journal of Social Psychology*, 134(6), 783–92.

Wann, D. L., Schinner, J., and Keenan, B. L. (2001) "Males' impressions of female fans and nonfans: there really is 'something about Mary'," *North American Journal of Psychology,* 3(2), 183.

Wann, D., Schrader, P., and Wilson, A. M. (1999) "Sport fan motivation: questionnaire validation, comparisons by sport and relationship to athletic motivation," *Journal of Sport Behaviour*, March.

Wasserman, V., Rafaeli, A., and Kluger, A. (2000) "Aesthetic symbols as emotional cues," in S. Fineman (ed.), *Emotion in Organizations,* Sage, London, 140–65.

Wenner, L. A. and Gantz, W. (1989) "The audience experiences with sports on television," in L. Wenner (ed.), *Media, Sports and Society*, Newbury Park, Calif., Sage, 241–69.

Westerbeck, H. and Smith, A. (2003) *Sport Business in the Global Marketplace,* Basingstoke, Palgrave Macmillan.

Williams, J. (1996) "The new football in England and Sir John Hall's New Geordie Nation'," in S. Gehrmann (ed.), *Football and Regions in Europe*, Hamburg, LIT Verlag.

Williams, J. (2007) "Rethinking sports fandom: the case of European soccer," *Leisure Studies*, 26(2), 127–46.

Yip, G. S. (1989) "Global strategy … in a world of nations?" *Sloan Management Review*, Autumn, 29–41.

Index